Special Thanks

I would like to thank the following people for their love, laughs and support throughout this journey:

My brother Jeff, Dolly, The Cousins, Uncle Mike, Aunt Arlene, Debbie, Audley, Antionette, Allison, and Andre. Brent, Karan, Bryan, Tina, Dennis, Danielle, Sean, Shrubber, Andy, Matt C, Melissa, Anna, The Kelly Family, Kevin, and Dermot. Adelbert, Dean, Yvonne Z, Rae, Rebecca, Vicki P. My comedy family: Tommy D, Mike Conley, Greg Morton, Basile, Greg Smrdel, Jeff Blanchard, Paul Bond, Tammy Pescatelli, Charlie Weiner, Bill Benden, Tim Folger, Tim Harrison, Chuck Constanzo, Lucy, Tim, Jeff, Pete, Nidal and Chef Tony. My KISS Army family: Arlene, Carol, Steve, Christie, Nigel, Don, Carl, Adri, James and George. Those I've met in Higher Education: Sandra, Dr. Kuhn, Dr. Padak, Stephanie, Charlene, Lauren P, Phyllis, Lawrence, Liz, Heather, Deb, Peggy, Mo and Jackie. Stow Municipal Court: Judge Kim Hoover, Beth, Steve, Judge Lisa

Coates, Jon, and Aaron. All those who have been on The Magic of Life Board: Jack, Andy, Christine, Jon, Shirley, Jacki, Erin, Chelsea, Wally, Lee, and Nate. David Schwensen, David Coleman, Rob Einhorn. All the schools, colleges, military bases, and Tina from NE Ohio MADD who have given me the opportunity to present *The Magic of Life*. My incredible manager GG Greg for helping me make a difference. Finally, my awesome writing coach, Mary Anna who pushed me to "paint the scene."

Book cover: Rae Staton,PRSTATONphotography

The Magic of Life:

A Son's Story of Hope after Tragedy, Grief and a Speedo

by

Michael Gershe

I hope You Enjoy
the book.

Michael Gershe

3/4/2021

Proceeds of this book go to The Magic of Life Foundation 501 (C) (3)

www.themagicoflife.org

In Memory

For my parents, Barbara and Martin Gershe, who gave me life and the opportunity to follow my dreams. I hope to continue making you proud in all that I do.

For my Aunt Sue who made sure I was out having fun.

Dedication

To Dolly Morris who helped raise me to become the man I am today.

Table of Contents

Introduction

Chapter 1: Hello World!

Chapter 2: Tragedy Hits

Chapter 3: The Initial Reaction

Chapter 4: The Drunk Driver

Chapter 5: Hello Dolly

Chapter 6: A New Family is Born

Chapter 7: Dolly's Impact

Chapter 8: North to South

Chapter 9: Becoming Floridians

Chapter 10: Lessons from a Speedo

Chapter 11: Dr. Magic

Chapter 12: Hello Ohio, Goodbye Sunshine

Chapter 13: The Six Pack

Chapter 14: Fish out of water

Chapter 15: The Final Countdown

Chapter 16: I Graduated, Now What?

Chapter 17: Hello Akron

Chapter 18: "Hello Mom, it's me, Michael"

Chapter 19: Chasing Comedy and Flipping Burgers

Chapter 20: Turning 30 with a Kidney Stone

Chapter 21: Big John Kelly

Chapter 22: A Big Farewell

Chapter 23: Life after Big John

Chapter 24: The Magic of Life Program

Chapter 25: Role Models

Chapter 26: The Joy of Making a Difference

Chapter 27: The Impact of The Magic of Life

Chapter 28: "You're a 48-year-old orphan"

Chapter 29: Remembering Dad

Chapter 30: Missing Dad, Evading Grief

Chapter 31: Aunt Sue

Chapter 32: "Your Foundation is Broken"

Chapter 33: Fixing My Foundation

Introduction

In 2002, at age thirty-one, I was in the green room of the Akron Hilarities Comedy Club on State Road in Cuyahoga Falls, Ohio just minutes away from performing. The show's headliner, Greg Morton, an extremely funny comedian and super nice guy from Canada, and I were talking about our lives on a couch that would make any germophobe convulse from disgust. Only the best in comedy clubs. When he heard about my life as a survivor of a drunk driving crash that killed my mother and nearly me as an infant, he was stunned. Then, when he heard I was raised by my father and a Jamaican woman he said, "You have to write a book Michael, what a story!"

I smiled and nodded, "yeah, yeah, whatever." However, he was serious and persistent as he looked at me through his glasses. "You have to write a book! Promise me. Promise me!" He grabbed my hand to shake on the promise as the showroom manager, Jeff, made his pre-show introductions. Greg had a vice grip on my hand as I heard, "Now please welcome your host and opening act,

Michael Gershe." Greg was not letting go. The crowd awaited my arrival. I should have been on stage 20 seconds ago. Finally, I gave in and said, "I promise."

I have been presenting *The Magic of Life,* a fun, non-doom and gloom impaired driving/alcohol awareness program for almost 25 years. I have been performing comedy for the same amount of time. I have spoken at schools, colleges, military bases and courtrooms for DUI offenders. The program combines comedy, audience participation and my story, for a different educational, and inspirational message. My goal is to make people laugh, inspire them, and help prevent impaired driving so no one has to go through what I, or countless others, have experienced. Usually, on stage, I only have an hour to share my journey, which as a speaker is not enough time to share everything I would like with an audience. Although, some might say it is excessively too much time. Regardless, this book gives me the opportunity to share my entire journey with you including the good, the bad, and ugly.

The course of this book has changed in so many directions that it has left my head spinning at times. I did not want it to be just a self-help book or just a book about surviving a horrific car crash. I did not want it to be just about coping with grief either. I have had a unique life relationship with grief, which started when a drunk driver changed my life. In our current culture, grief and depression has been mentioned a lot, but more can be done to assist those in need. I believe my story could provide help to someone else who needs a positive message. I have experienced grief and depression through every stage of my life: as a child, a teen and an adult. I have battled the evils of depression and suicidal thoughts but yet, found a way to survive even when I did not think I could or would.

I want to share my journey with you. Not just how I created *The Magic of Life* program and the impact it's made, but how my life decisions led to who I have become. I was blessed with a sense of humor, which I call my "super power." It has gotten me in trouble at school, in meetings, and earned me a dirty look or two in a relationship. However, the majority of the time, whether it is onstage or off, it has brought laughs. I do not know how I could have survived this long without my sense of humor. I could have crawled into a bottle my entire life and played the "victim" card, but what fun would that have been? Something inside of me needs to hear a laugh on a daily basis. Ask any comedian and they will tell you that the ability of making someone laugh is an incredible natural high.

Over the years, like *The Magic of Life* program itself, I have evolved so much since I made that promise to Greg in that green room. When I submitted manuscript version 203 for a book review, I told my reviewer/writing coach, "I want to make sure that I'm not wasting my time, and this isn't just a big pile of crap." Fortunately, she did not feel that way and with her help, this book transformed into something that is part of my soul. I want to give you a front row seat, not only to my life, but also to what may go on in someone else's mind, body and spirit as they overcome tragedy in their life.

While I may seem like a happy-go-lucky guy, I have spent my life hiding behind my humor. For so long I was in denial over my depression. As a typical male, I thought, I did not need any help. Later in life, I found out that asking for help was not a weakness, but a strength. Despite all our difficulties in life, how we cope with the darkness is vital to our survival. It is my hope that by reading this, you will laugh and cry with me. I want you to enjoy the journey, but also gain something new and exciting about yourself at the same time. I want you to understand just how precious your life is, not only to you, but also to those who love you.

Despite barely surviving that car crash, I went on to become a collegiate swimmer, comedian, speaker, and author. I know how lucky I am to be here and experience a memorable life. As a proud member of the KISS Army, I have seen the band in concert numerous times since 1988 and met the band on several occasions. I had the honor of attending a Medal of Honor Ceremony and made countless of people laugh. Most of all, I have made a difference by sharing my story of being a survivor of a drunk driving crash. I never want anyone to go through what my family has gone through with something that is so preventable. Drunk driving does not have to happen and quite frankly, it needs to stop!

We all have powerful stories to share, this just happens to be mine. At the time of finally finishing this manuscript in January 2019, I am about to perform once again with my dear friend Greg Morton. Talk about comedic timing! I thank you for reading and if you really do not like it, you can blame Greg who made me promise all those years ago. I have his phone number, email, PlayStation username and all his social media links…

Here's to finding The Magic of Life together,

Michael Gershe

Founder/Director,

The Magic of Life Foundation

www.themagicoflife.org

Greg Morton and I performing again at the Funny Stop Comedy Club in Cuyahoga Falls, OH 1/19/19

Chapter 1

Hello World!

I was born on July 24, 1970, in Suffern New York, to Barbara and Martin Gershe; their second and favorite son. My brother Jeff entered the world three years before me. We lived in a nice two-story house that my parents built in Spring Valley after living in an apartment for a few years. Spring Valley is a pleasant, quiet middle-class suburban neighborhood, an hour north of New York City. My parents were two young people, excited to start their family.

Between July 24th, and September 19th, my father recorded our lives together. Here is a description of the video I show in *The Magic of Life*: (https://www.youtube.com/watch?v=NS33fsu70dQ&t=2s)

A young mother is in a chair holding her newborn baby during his bris. The film is in color, but the picture is a bit grainy. You can see family members surrounding her and the new addition. The videographer is the boys' father. He points the camera at the baby's grandparents, then the Rabbi, and finally sweeps by others in the picture, capturing the family giving the young baby support before the ceremony begins. The young mother smiles with pride, comforting her son, as only a mother can. The film transitions to a new scene. The mother, wearing a summer dress with a flowery pattern stands at the top of the stairs outside the back deck of her home. She carries her sleeping newborn down the steps into the family's backyard. She holds the infant up to the camera and smiles, her eyes hidden behind large black sunglasses. The mother stops by a metal playground structure in the backyard. Her husband continues to film as the baby's older brother comes into the picture and gives him a tender kiss on the check.

The three-year-old proceeds to show off his keen gymnastic abilities by hanging on the playground bars while the mother watches, still holding her sleeping son in her arms. The frame jumps to the mother kneeling in the grass holding her infant. The older child does a somersault from left to right. She applauds his effort, while carefully cradling the newborn. The older son does another somersault towards his mother as she looks on in delight, just enjoying the moment with her children. One can only wonder by watching the video now how the older son never grew up to be a professional tumbler.

He blows a kiss towards his father behind the camera and then turns to his mother innocently. Perhaps he asks to hold his baby brother, promising to be very careful. His mother instructs him to sit on the grass facing his father who films the action. She tells her son to be careful with his baby brother as she places the infant into his tiny arms. Like any good older sibling whose job is to protect the younger one, he falls over onto his left side. The boy lays on his side as his baby brother tumbles out of his arms and onto the grass. The older brother laughs and looks at his sibling. Cut. Fade to black.

Shortly after this home movie, our lives were changed forever.

My parents wedding day, December 19, 1964

Chapter 2
Tragedy Hits

On September 19, 1970, my father was driving us home from Long Island. We were visiting family friends who attended my parent's wedding. It was just a typical drive. My father approached the intersection of Rt.45 and New Hempstead Road around 11 p.m., less than a mile from our home. My brother Jeff was sleeping in the backseat, my mother was sitting in the front middle seat, and I was in an infant carrier next to her by the passenger door. In 1970, we did not use seat belts like today because 99.99% of the time the buckles were stuffed between the seat. As our light turned green, my father gently tapped the gas and proceeded through the intersection. As he crossed the intersection, a car from the right drove through his red light. My father did not remember seeing the bright headlights engulf our vehicle. He lost consciousness when the two cars collided.

Back then, they built strong cars out of actual steel that would last through generations, not like today where a shopping cart causes $5,000 worth of damage in a parking lot. On that fateful night, a drunk driver t-boned our car. He hit us with such force that our car rammed into a pole, splitting the front all the way to the dashboard. The impact was so loud; it woke up the neighbors. Our car was a mangled piece of twisted metal.

Suddenly, my father regained consciousness. He had no idea how long he was out. He paused for a minute and began to process what had happened. He screamed, "Where is my baby? Where is my baby? Where is my baby?"

Patrolman Eberling of the Ramapo Town Police got the call at 11:06 p.m. He was told an ambulance was enroute. When he arrived on the scene, he started first-aid for the injured parties. Patrolman Ronald Chamberlain arrived on the scene at about 11:13 p.m. and assisted with first-aid. Three minutes later, the Hillcrest Fire Department pulled up next to what was left of our car. I asked my childhood friend, Adelbert Duyvelaar, a lieutenant with the Hialeah Fire Department, in South Florida, what goes through a first responder's mind when arriving to a crash scene. He said, "Lots of emotions go through our minds, but first and foremost, we have to keep our wits about us because if we don't, people die. We put our emotions aside, so we can do our jobs. Once all is said and done, we have a chance to think about what just happened."

After arriving on scene, the firefighters found my father, mother and brother in that twisted mess, but they could not find me, since I did not make any noise. I honestly do not even know how they knew I was in the car. Ten or fifteen minutes later, the first responders made a startling discovery. There I was, crushed between the mangled passenger door and dashboard. They carefully extracted me from the debris. When my father finally saw me, I was wrapped in a blanket and held by a first responder or a neighbor. He could not determine the extent of my injuries. Little did we know, that was for the best. An ambulance transported the four of us to Ramapo General Hospital.

Miraculously, Jeff had no injuries. Not even a scratch on him. Perhaps it was divine intervention, or pure luck since he was sleeping in the back seat that allowed him to escape unscathed. My father was slightly banged up. He received several stitches above his eyebrow, on the right side of his face and nose from the broken glass. My mother was rushed into surgery. She suffered head injuries from either the windshield, the dashboard, or possibly the rear-view mirror.

Then there was me. If you have held an infant before, you know how delicate they are. There are approximately 305 bones in a newborn's body. They're mostly cartilage and still take time to completely form into bone. Ossification turns the cartilage into 206 bones as you grow up. Nearly every bone in my body was broken. My skull was fractured like the letter "U" from one side to the other. When my father asked the doctor, "How is my baby?" The doctor somberly replied, "Your baby is touch and go. He will have to be observed closely. We simply do not know if he will survive." The anxiety my father was experiencing had to be so overwhelming. His wife was in surgery fighting for her life and his infant son was also on the edge of death. As a parent and spouse, it had to be the worst nightmare anyone can experience.

My injuries were so severe that I was airlifted to Good Samaritan Hospital in Suffern so I could be treated by trauma specialists. Now that I think about it, I had a helicopter ride that I do not remember, and I would like another one! Years later, my Uncle Charlie said, "When we saw you in the hospital, you had no neck. It was just your head sitting on top of your shoulders. It was horrible, just horrible." My father, in one of the few times he talked about the crash once told me, "You were broken, your body was like Jell-O."

I have two two-inch scars on each ankle and one on the inside of my right elbow from all the blood transfusions I received to help keep me alive. My Aunt Susan told me, "It was sad to see you get all those transfusions. I even lost count of how many you received that scary night. To see those scars now always reminds me of that nightmare."

My tiny body had to be strapped down on a board most of the time so my bones would heal properly. Doctors could not put me in a cast since I was mostly cartilage. They believed this was the best way for me to heal.

My father told me, "The doctors did not have a clue if you would survive, much alone recover. They never treated an infant with such severe injuries. We had no idea if you would be normal, physically or mentally. When you started to walk, I thought you would fall apart."

Due to the fractured skull, I had to be taken to the hospital for months afterward to make sure I did not have any brain damage. Now, I can attest that I do not have any, but some friends and probably ex-girlfriends would likely argue that point. It is strange to look at the scars from the blood transfusions now and not remember how I got them. I remember the one from Bobby Stewart's braces on my right bicep as we wrestled before a swim meet, but these three that saved my life? Not at all. Maybe that is a good thing.

When I started speech therapy years later, we wondered if it was related to fractured skull or just normal growing pains that come with childhood development. Nevertheless, I had to deal with the physical and mental effects of the crash for the rest of my life. Despite growing up to become a competitive swimmer, we did not know if my numerous injuries were because of over-training or some lingering effect of the car crash.

My mother, Barbara, the second and youngest daughter in her family, grew up in a tiny one-bedroom in

Brooklyn. She and her sister would sleep in the living room until they moved to a two-bedroom apartment later in childhood. She was a quiet kid who never got into trouble. She eventually became a schoolteacher. As a loving wife and mother, she enjoyed planting flowers in the backyard. On the morning of September 20, 1970, she succumbed to her injuries from the crash.

According to the police report, Officer Eberling received a call from Ramapo General Hospital at 6:10 a.m. My mother had passed. I never could bring myself to ask my father if she died in surgery or if she ever regained consciousness. My mother was killed by a drunk driver and left behind a husband, two young sons, a sister and parents. My father may have suffered minor physical injuries, but his mental scars would never heal. They were married for only six years until a drunk driver destroyed a wonderful life.

My mother was laid to rest in the Gershe family plot on Long Island. My brother shared three years with her. I had just under eight weeks. I often wonder about our time together. Did I let her sleep through the night? Did I make her smile and laugh during those eight weeks? I am forty-eight years old and do not have a single memory of my mother due to a drunk driver. Our family was now shattered. How would we continue after this?

Taken the same day as the video was filmed.

The only picture I have with my mother.

Chapter 3

The Initial Reaction

My Aunt Susan was living in Brooklyn, with her parents at the time of the crash when the phone in the apartment rang late in the evening. Upon hanging up the phone, my grandmother told her, "Martin and the family were in a car crash. You need to get dressed right away. We're going to the hospital."

During that hour and twenty-minute drive from Brooklyn to Spring Valley, my Aunt Susan recalled how nervous she was as she sat in the backseat. "We didn't talk much on that drive, as we had lumps in our throats, not knowing what to expect once we got to the hospital"

When they arrived, my grandparents quickly disappeared to talk with the doctors. My aunt found Jeff's hospital room. He was lying in a crib, alone and crying. She picked him up and held him close. He stopped crying after a while. My father and brother stayed overnight in the hospital while my grandparents along with my aunt drove back to Brooklyn to get a few things so they could stay at our house until things settled.

Once we came home from the hospital, my grandmother and aunt stayed with us. They cooked and took care of the house. A nurse was hired to take care of me since I was healing on that special board. After a couple of weeks, my aunt returned to Brooklyn and only came up to the house on the weekends with my grandfather who worked during the week in the city. My aunt does not remember much of my mother's family involvement after the crash, but she does recall my mother's parents coming up on the weekends as well. I never got to know my maternal grandparents. They passed within a relatively short time after my mother's death.

Years ago, I sat down with my mother's sister, Arlene, to discuss more about this time from her perspective, but realized after a few questions that the memory was just too painful. While I wanted to know more, I could not put her through it. Dealing with grief is such a delicate situation that never ends. While I wanted answers, I was acutely aware and empathetic of her feelings.

One of the saddest memories my Aunt Susan remembers is when my father finally went back to work. You cannot expect a three-year-old to understand or cope with such a traumatic event. Upon hearing how my brother reacted, she felt bad for him. I had it easy being an infant. When my father left for work, Jeff would be sleeping, but would cry hysterically for what seemed like hours when he woke up and saw my father was gone. They tried another tactic. Each morning they would wake Jeff up before my father left, but after he would kiss Jeff goodbye, Jeff would grab onto my father's foot and cry hysterically for hours once again. "The memory of a three-year old Jeffrey on the stairs pulling on Martin's arm and crying hysterically each morning is still burned into my brain," my Aunt Sue said.

If the car crash happened today, grief counselors would have been summoned to the hospital for my brother and father immediately, but not in 1970. The anxiety my brother experienced when my father left for work had to be tremendous, thinking he would never see our dad again. Just like our mother. He already bonded with both of them. It had to be so strange not to see our mother anymore. Today there are many ways to help a kid cope with grief, but then? Not so much.

Surviving the car crash may have been pure luck but healing mentally would be a lifelong struggle. After about a month of assistance from family members, there was talk of how my father would manage with Jeff and I when the nurse was no longer required for my care. My grandmother, also, wanted to return to her life in Brooklyn. Although there were plenty of single mothers around during our time, it was much rarer for a man to be doing the same in 1970.

While my Aunt Sue was not included in the discussions, she was aware of the conversations taking place regarding a "live-in" employee to take care of me and Jeff while our father worked. We were not a rich family by any means, but we needed the help. Ads were placed in a local newspaper and my grandmother made up the search committee for this important position. Interviews were held, and one thing was certain, our lives would never be the same again. From something so tragic came something magical for all of us. We just did not know it yet. A guardian angel would be sent to us, perhaps from my mother. I would not believe in such fate if it did not happen to me.

Chapter 4

The Drunk Driver

My grandparents would not let my father see the remains of the car. My father told me once, "They did not even want me in the courtroom during the trial. They knew that if I was in there, I would have strangled the guy." As I got older, I always wanted my father to voluntarily talk about the crash. I wanted to know everything. I knew how tough it was for him, but yet, never understood the magnitude of the pain and why he still, after all these years, could not talk about it. Much of what I know comes from the Ramapo Police report I obtained in my mid-30s.

After the ambulance left the scene, Patrolman Eberling spoke with Harvey, the driver of the other car. Harvey refused medical treatment. He was sitting in the driver's seat when asked if he was the driver, he told the officer, "No, John (his friend) was the driver. I was the passenger in the car." There were three people in the car, Harvey, his friend John and John's wife. He continued, "We were going south on Rt. 45 to the Ramapo General Hospital because John was sick and wanted to see a doctor. The next thing I knew, I was sitting in the car on the side of the road."

When the ambulance returned to the scene, Harvey decided to go to the hospital. The officer noticed a strong smell of alcohol on his breath, bloodshot eyes, and very slurred speech. At 11:50 p.m., approximately an hour after the crash, the officer questioned John's wife who said she "did not know what happened because she was in the backseat with her husband." He then spoke with John who gave him the same statement.

This made me so angry for many, many years. The drunk driver lied, HE LIED! Even as I write these words, I am angry. What type of person lies and throws his friend under the bus in a tragic car crash? This person does not care about other people. If I was his friend, upon hearing what he told the officer, I would have been livid. Wouldn't you?

Around 2:00 a.m., Lt. John Von Ohlsen arrived at the hospital to assist with the investigation. Patrolman Eberling explained to the lieutenant that he couldn't determine who was actually driving the car since Harvey said he wasn't driving, and John said Harvey was driving.

Finally, at 2:20 a.m., in the hallway of the hospital, Harvey admitted to Lt. Von Ohlsen that he was driving and lied at the time of the accident because his license had been revoked. Harvey was placed under arrest for driving while intoxicated, reporting a false incident, and operating a vehicle with a revoked license. He was read his rights and agreed to a blood test. His license had been revoked three years prior. THREE YEARS! How many times have you heard of a drunk driver operating a motor vehicle with a suspended license?

At 2:54 a.m., his blood was taken and registered a .10. It was also at this time that Harvey signed his physical condition report taken by Officer Eberling that stated the following:

Ability to walk: Moving in circles

Ability to stand: Swaying

Speech: Confused

Breath: Odor of alcohol beverage – strong

Condition of hair: Mussed

Condition of eyes: Bloodshot

Condition of face: Flushed

Attitude: Combative

Have you been drinking? Yes

What? Beer

How much? Six pack

At 3:20 a.m., Lt. Von Ohlsen continued questioning Harvey at headquarters and his rights were once again explained to him. Harvey finally agreed, at 3:45 a.m., to give the officer a voluntary statement of the facts leading up to the accident. Lt. Von Ohlsen contacted the assistant district attorney at 6:33 a.m. to inform him of my mother's death. Upon learning this new development, the assistant DA told him to charge Harvey with criminally negligent homicide. He was also charged with false reporting of an incident, operating vehicle while intoxicated, and operating vehicle with a suspended license. He signed his "acknowledgment of rights" form at 3:25 a.m. Harvey was fingerprinted shortly after and allowed to make his phone call. He was held at the Rockland County Jail in lieu of a $6,000 bail.

My father said Harvey could not pay his bail, so he stayed in jail. The notice of final disposition was dated June 8th, 1971 where Harvey was sent to state prison for a maximum of three years. Because he could not pay his bail and remained in jail since the crash, he did not serve all three years from the date of sentencing. The pain this man caused was not even worth three years in the eyes of justice. This hardly seems fair, especially when he knowingly lied to the police. Drunk driving is not a mistake, it is a choice. On that night, he chose to drive drunk, killing my mother and changing many lives.

In late August 2016, I had the opportunity to share my story with Gene Simmons of KISS. Gene asked me, "How many years of prison did the man who killed your mother get?" "Three years with time served." Gene shook his head, as his mouth opened (without the tongue!) in disbelief. That's pretty much the same response everyone has.

Chapter 5

Hello Dolly

As my father balanced grieving for his wife, working to support us, and trying to raise Jeff and I, my grandparents believed that a live-in employee would be the best thing for the family. It was October 1970 when my grandmother, Nana, placed an ad in the newspaper for a part-time position. People started to respond. My father was not a part of the hiring process and the applicants came and went from my grandparent's apartment. To my grandmother, it did not matter what religion or race each person was. Her only goal was to hire someone reliable who would take the best care of her grandsons. It can be somewhat daunting for a stranger to break down a Jewish grandmother's defense, especially when it comes to her grandsons, but one woman managed to do just that.

Dolly Morris (who is so humble that she did not want her name being used in this book - maybe I embarrass her!) was born Myrtle Morris in Maypen, Jamaica. She came from a large family with four siblings. She hated the name Myrtle because kids would call her "Myrtle the Turtle," so she eventually changed her name to Dolly. She was so small as a child. Her parents would say she looked like a little doll. Dolly was a natural name for her.

Prior to coming to New York, Dolly lived in England where she was the first policewoman for Scotland Yard. She worked mostly with juveniles and also studied nursing at the same time. As fate would have it that October, she was visiting her sister in New York (who also was studying nursing.) She recalls how she arrived during Halloween and saw cars with eggs on them. "I hated America. I didn't want to stay at all. I almost slipped on the pavement outside from the eggs. New York was so dirty compared to England," Dolly said.

While she was planning to return to Jamaica to finish nursing school, her mother convinced her to stay and enjoy her vacation with her sister. Dolly had three months of vacation time, so she considered getting a part-time job to make some money. Dolly saw my grandmother's ad and called to find out more information. My grandmother told her the job was basically taking care of a toddler and infant, preparing meals for their father while he worked. Dolly would have weekends off. Our house was over an hour from the city and for Dolly it would seem like another world away from where she was staying with her sister.

Dolly and my grandmother set up an interview in Brooklyn, but Dolly never showed up because she could not get a ride. She was also afraid of taking the subway by herself since she was still a stranger in a strange land. I get it, the subway system in New York can be quite intimidating. Dolly did not call my grandmother back to let her know she could not make it or to reschedule. Despite this, she thought about the job for the next two weeks.

Dolly still wanted a part-time job. Without realizing it the same ad from a few weeks back, she called the number listed in the advertisement.

"Didn't you call before?" my grandmother asked her caller.

"Yes, I did, and I'm sorry but I could not get a ride for the interview. I'm still interested if the job is still open." Dolly said. My grandmother was desperate since no one wanted the job.

"Yes, it is still available, and I would love to meet with you about it," my grandmother told her. They arranged to meet on Friday evening at the house in Spring Valley to make things easier for Dolly. Her sister could go with her, helping her navigate New York City's public transportation. She and her sister took the number 2 train to Port Authority and the last bus to Spring Valley.

By the time Dolly got to my grandmother's home in Brooklyn, she was completely drenched and miserable from a rainstorm. My grandmother offered Dolly some tea to help warm her up. Dolly was so excited about the tea, because coming from England, "the English know how to do tea!" She pepped up and was ready for that tea to warm up her bones. Despite her eagerness, Dolly was unsure if my grandmother could make tea that she was used to in England.

My grandmother handed her the teacup. Dolly expected her dark, English style tea, but what she saw in front of her almost reduced her to tears! My grandmother gave her "milky water" instead of "real tea." Dolly assumed that the tea was bad. She thought my grandmother dipped the bag in water for a few seconds and just added milk. When Dolly told me this story decades later, she laughed about it, but on that day, she nearly cried. In complete Dolly fashion, she showed my grandmother how to make a good cup of tea and thus their bonding began.

The pair sat and talked over proper tea. Dolly thought it was strange my grandmother said the job was taking care of the boys during the day and cooking for their father. "What happened to their mother?" she asked.

"Their mother was killed in a car accident a few weeks ago," my grandmother replied. Her voice choking as she fought back tears. Dolly's heart sank like an anchor upon hearing that. They sat together, sharing a silent moment as the heavy revelation hung in the air.

"Would you like to meet the baby, Michael?" my grandmother asked, changing the subject.

"Of course, I would," Dolly replied.

The pair ascended the steps to my room.

"Michael broke all of his bones and fractured his skull in the crash," my grandmother added.

(Dolly told me years later that I had to be picked up with a pillow wrapped around me to protect my bones that were still healing).

Dolly walked toward the crib. She told me, "I fell in love with you right away. You were all smiles, laughing and cute." She stuck her finger in between the crib bars, and I latched onto it right away. I didn't let go!

"I knew right there that God had brought me to your family. I knew that this is where I was needed most," Dolly said.

First of all, I was a baby. Of course, I was cute. I've seen Dolly around babies, she loves them to pieces. When she is around them, you can't tear her away from one. There isn't a baby on this planet that she would not adore and take care of, but I'd like to think it was my cuteness that sealed the deal. She once told me, "I didn't do it for the glory, God chose me for your family."

They started to walk downstairs to discuss the job when my grandmother stopped on the landing. "You have to take the job, we are desperate, and Michael already likes you," she begged Dolly. My father and brother had just returned from the bank and my grandmother introduced Dolly to 3-year-old Jeffrey.

"Jeffrey, this lady will be taking care of you."

Jeff looked at Dolly and then at our father and replied, while shaking his head no. "Hey Dad, us guys don't need anyone, right Dad? We're big men, we don't need help, she's here for the baby, right? She's here for Michael. We guys gotta stick together!"

But we did need help. All three of us.

Dolly was hired in November 1970 and has been a part of the family ever since. You may call it destiny, but I think God and my mother worked together to bring her to us.

Chapter 6

A New Family is Born

"Your mother's name was never mentioned," Dolly told me years later. "Your grandmother would shush people if they said her name. She would ask 'why did it have to happen to my son?' My father was struggling to get up and get out of the house on a daily basis and rightly so. With his wife gone, her death was not a topic of conversation in our home. "Your grandparents would not talk about it. I thought your father should be checked out," Dolly said.

My father's wife, our mother, was gone and not one person suggested counseling of any sort back then. Getting men to admit they needed counseling is tough enough today, but back then? Forget about it. Plus, I doubt my father would have gone. He remained pretty silent about the crash throughout my entire life. Dolly observed him as "not being there," for at least a year as he wouldn't really speak at all. Eventually he started to put one foot in front of the other, struggling through the grieving process to do what was best for me and my brother.

"Your father was a bit wary of me at first," Dolly said. "Who was this woman? Who is she to feed my boys? Who is she to spend time with them as I worked during the day?" But he didn't really talk about it. Everyone just bottled up their feelings about my mother, which became a family trend with death that repeated itself throughout my life.

The former police officer from Scotland Yard would sleep in my room and said I would often peer through my crib to watch her sleep. And if she left, I would cry. Somehow, I always knew when she was leaving for the weekend. One day she put her fingers in my crib. I latched onto them and pulled myself up to standing. My father got a bit nervous and said, "He is not ready to stand yet, he is still healing from the crash." He was still incredibly scared of my condition and recovery since the doctors could not give him a definite answer about my prognosis. I eventually grew normally except I think my wrists stopped growing at some point because my father would have to put extra holes in watch bands in order for them to fit me. I have the wrists of a five-year old. Anyway, Dolly was so excited when I stood up.

"Look!" she exclaimed, "He's ready, he's standing!" Somehow, she always knew when I was ready to do something in life.

According to my Aunt Sue, Dolly was extremely competent, and the entire family worked hard to make her feel welcome and part of the family. My mother's supportive four sisters included Dolly in all family functions. Dolly, however, did not have a permanent visa. My grandfather worked hard to sponsor her so she could successfully obtain her permanent visa "and stay with Martin and the boys." My grandparents were extremely happy with her work, she even got a raise.

Dolly though, was ready to go back to home after a few months. Technically, she was still on "vacation" and wanted to resume her schooling to become a nurse. She asked my grandparents if they could hire someone else, but my grandparents would not hear of it. They saw how, in just a short period of time, Dolly was making such a huge impact with the family and was now, irreplaceable. Besides, you cannot really argue with a Jewish grandmother, they always get their way - ALWAYS!

My grandfather was adamant that Dolly continue to work with us. In such a short time, Dolly formed incredible bonds with every member of our family. Deep down, Dolly knew she couldn't leave. So, Dolly got a work permit, allowing her to continue working with our family. True to his word, my grandfather knew a lawyer who helped expedite the paperwork. This way, Dolly wouldn't be working illegally. Dolly flew back to Jamaica to get all her papers completed and soon after, it was a done deal - she was going to stay with us a bit longer.

I had the easiest transition with Dolly and the crash since I was only an infant, but Jeff's transition was more problematic. Jeff, according to Dolly, really struggled after the car crash. Along with freaking out when our Dad left for work, he would also have horrible nightmares. He had some challenges with Dolly too. Jeff thought he was a "big boy" at three and a half years old. To him, Dolly was a stranger so why should he listen to her? One day, while my father was at work, he told her she was not the boss and that she was not in charge. Oh, out of the mouths of babes!

Shortly after that, Dolly told my father, "In order for things to work, I must have control during the day, and you cannot change those decisions when you come home." She told me, "Your father would come home from work and sometimes changed things which caused a little conflict, but after a while, he accepted what I was doing." Because my father agreed with her, Jeff was not happy.

One night as Dolly was preparing us for bed her sister called. Unlike today, we actually had to go the phone in 1970 that hung on the wall with a cord so long you would get tangled up like a cowboy wrangling a bull. She stopped helping Jeff get ready for bed, thinking our grandmother would finish the job. Eventually, Jeff refused my grandmother's help and sat down by Dolly's feet in the kitchen while she was on the phone. She was holding the phone in one hand and me in the other. Jeff sat there and told my grandmother, "I will wait for Dolly." It took a few months for them to bond for life, but Dolly bonded with everyone. She just had a way about her.

Another favorite story that Dolly likes to share about Jeff is a good one. One day he came home from school with a black eye. "What happened to your eye, Jeff?" Dolly asked. "Who did that to you?"

"Another student punched me today," Jeff replied.

As she put ice on his eye, she told him, "You have to learn to defend yourself against a bully. Stand up for yourself. Don't come home again with another black eye, okay?" The next day the school called and said Jeff gave another student a bloody nose. My father was not too happy to hear the news, but Dolly told him "He has to stand up for himself or the kids will never stop." As always, she was right.

Rumor has it that a couple of years later Jeff was being picked on in our driveway by a neighborhood kid. The story, according to Dolly, is that little me picked up a baseball bat, raised it over my head and was about to slam it down on the kid's skull when Dolly saw me and yelled, "MICHAEL!!!" That caused me to drop the bat and thus not having a criminal record at the age of three. Obviously, I have no recollection of this event, but Dolly *loves* sharing it. A lot.

She also loves sharing the story of the time we dropped my father off at the airport for one of his business trips to Germany. We were at a Chinese restaurant with my grandparents and I, like a typical toddler, was banging my silverware on the table. Suddenly I stood up with a knife, turned around and started to pound the man in the booth behind us on the head as if I was the next Ringo Starr! My family looked on in horror but could not stop laughing. Thus, my future as a professional drummer was no more. I love hearing Dolly share stories of us from back then because, one, I love her laugh as she shares it, and two, she seems happy.

For some reason, I do not remember other fond memories like dumping a bucket of water on Dolly's head when she cleaned the stairs or hitting her in the head with a toy, she was trying to take away from me. Let's be honest, when you try to take a toy away from a toddler, your life is at risk.

One-time Dolly took me to the mall with another parent and her kid when I was three. They decided to watch each other's kid while the other shopped. Seems like a good plan, right? Well, when it was the other parent's turn to watch me, I wandered away. Dolly was so frantic because she didn't want to be the one to tell my father that she lost his son. The other parent told Dolly, "It's his fault for walking away." Dolly who was cemented as our mother figure at this point, yelled at her, "You were supposed to be watching him, how do you let a three-year-old just walk away?!" When they eventually found me, I was in the security office eating a huge lollipop. Dolly was relieved to find me and started to laugh when she saw I was okay with the lollipop. But c'mon, I could have been on the back of a milk carton due to someone's lack of attention.

Dolly gave me love and apparently, I tormented her in my earlier days in New York, seems fair, right? As she reflected on those early days, she told me, "I had so much fun with you kids, so much fun!"

Dolly with Jeff and I outside our house in Spring Valley, NY

Chapter 7
Dolly's Impact

We were quickly becoming Dolly's sons, not just "two boys she took care of." I find it interesting that we were not that far removed from the civil rights movement, but in our family, race was never an issue. My family did not care she was black, and her family did not care we were white. Everyone got along because people just cared that Jeff and I were taken care of as if we were her own children. It is amazing how tragedy can bring people together, and in our case, we could not have asked for a better silver lining.

While I have spent many days of my life trying to rationalize my mother's death, having Dolly in my life gave me much comfort and support. Growing up, people would assume she was our "nanny," "maid," or "housekeeper" but they didn't understand our dynamic. Even today when I explain how Dolly was my mother, people still want to say she was my nanny. They just didn't get the significance. And maybe they never will.

My mother gave me life. Her death gave me purpose. Dolly, along with my father, taught me how to live and helped me to become the person I am today. You can thank her, or blame her, take your pick. It was funny, at least to me, that whenever I did something good at school, she would wait for my father to come home and say, "Guess what our son did today!" But, if I did something bad, it was, "Guess what *your* son did today?" Wait a minute. You cannot have it both ways.

I know how lucky we are to have each other. Without her, I shudder to think how I would have turned out. My father was never the same after the crash and there was no way he could have raised us alone.

We were becoming a regular family, my father and Dolly raised Jeff and me as two parents. Dolly taught me about unconditional love and what the human spirit is capable of doing. She sacrificed her dreams of becoming a nurse, even when she had a chance to leave in the early days, she stayed because we were a family. Later on, like typical families, if I went to my father and asked him for something, his response was, "Go ask Dolly." Dolly's response would be "Go ask your father." What kid doesn't love that "go ask the other parent game" growing up?

Over time, Dolly and my father formed more than just a work relationship. They formed a personal relationship. At one point, she tried to get him to date. I think he had enough of dating when one woman wanted to send me and Jeff to boarding school! Jeff, I can understand, but me? To me it was quite normal to see them as a couple because that is all I knew in life. Out of something so tragic, this beautiful thing arose.

Dolly supported our dreams, defended us, and most of all, loved us as her own children. One could never win an argument with her, either. Years ago, when I moved into a new place, she wanted to buy me a sofa bed instead of a regular couch, which I wanted. I knew money was tight for her and my father. I protested and said no, it's too much money. We argued and she said, "We are family, we are blood, and if I want to sacrifice something for you, then I will." Guess who got a sofa bed?

Dolly loves us unconditionally in what started out as a $40 per week part-time job in 1970 and that turned into a full-time motherhood role. She may have started as an employee, but quickly became family. I do not think anyone would have thought at the initial interview with my grandmother and that horrible tea, that this would be the outcome. As I said earlier, Dolly has been there for the good, the bad and the ugly. I remember when I got my heart broken for the first time and the woman said, "My family didn't think you were right for me." Dolly was offended because how dare someone say her son was not good enough for her.

Dolly's response was defiant, "Well, to hell with her and her family!" You do not mess with Dolly's boys.

If my mother was not killed and Dolly did not come into my life, I may not have believed in fate or that there is a higher power. How is it that from the death of my mother, that a white Jewish family would be saved by a Jamaican woman who just wanted a part-time job while she was on vacation in New York? How does that happen? Here was a woman who sacrificed her dreams, and her goals, for us. What does that tell you about her? Can you imagine if society had a lot more of Dolly's in it? What a much better place it would be.

She stepped in and said, "I will help raise these boys!" Only a person so unselfish of her own dreams would do something like this. Dolly is our mother, pure and simple. When she introduces us to people, she says, "These are my sons." Not sure what goes through people's minds when they hear that. Honestly, it doesn't really matter to me. We never thought, "Hey, we are white, and she is black." We are family. It was a normal way for Jeff and me to grow up. We never thought twice about it.

I believe that Dolly was the only person who could have stepped into this role. It was an impossible situation, but yet, as she said, "This is where I was needed." And I am so grateful she thought that. She raised us as her own and it takes a special person to see that this was not just a "job", but it was her calling. It was fate and one that made me believe in guardian angels. Dolly not only impacted my family, but with everyone she met. Her passion is tennis and she developed numerous leagues for children and adults. Good luck trying to get her off the phone if you start talking tennis! Her laugh is heavenly, and her heart is of gold. I would be lost without her.

Top: Dolly and me at Disney World

Bottom: A rare picture of Dolly in the pool

This is where I get my immaturity. 11/24/18

Chapter 8

North to South

"Let's live in South Florida and escape the New York winters," I told my father in early 1975.

Okay, so it didn't exactly go that way, I mean I was only four, but we did move to Miami because my father was going to go into business with his cousin. The only memory I have of the house in New York is competing in a potato sack race in the backyard for a birthday party. I don't even remember starting swim lessons at our local community center while we lived in New York. I wonder what it was like for my father to leave behind the house he built with my mother. We went from a big two-story house into a small two-bedroom apartment right off of US 1 and 144th street in Miami.

We spent two years in that apartment. Jeff and I shared a room with bunk beds while my Dad and Dolly shared the other room. I was on the bottom bunk. Jeff was up on top since he was older. I have fond memories living there and going to Vineland Elementary school. I especially remember standing outside for the bus when it snowed on January 19th, 1977. After living in Ohio for over 20 years now, I know what real snow is, but back then, it was like a blizzard in the sunshine state. I did not recall snow in New York, but it was such a historic day in Miami, how could I forget?

Sometimes it is the simple encounters that can become the most profound. I remember a school assembly where some fifth graders dressed up like KISS and lip-synced *Shout it Out Loud* while wielding wooden tennis racquets. Around this time, my brother was listening to KISS as well. I found their songs to be catchy and was really intrigued by the band's appearance. (Who wouldn't be?) Jeff eventually "grew out" of his KISS Phase and hopped onto the *Genesis* train. Not me. I grew up to be a devout member of the KISS Army. How one goes from KISS to Genesis is beyond me. He eventually became a Jimmy Buffet "Parrot Head." Perhaps Jeff is adopted!

As a child, I would often sit in our tiny kitchen daydreaming instead of eating my breakfast in a timely fashion. This habit would cause me to almost miss the bus. We only had one car that my dad drove to work. Dolly would set an egg timer and say, "You better eat your breakfast before that bell goes off or you're in big trouble." It's no wonder I am a fast eater to this day. Jeff and I kid with her now and say, "The punishment you gave us back then would be considered child abuse today." We never got in trouble at school because the punishment at home from her would be way worse than anything the school could give us. At least if I got detention I could sit in my chair. I wouldn't be able to sit at home, that's for sure!

When we were not at school, Jeff and I were swimming. We found a home at Sheeler-Winton Swim Club, a swimming mecca at the time in Miami. It was founded and coached by Al Sheeler and his wife Dot. Coach Sheeler had a perpetual tan and commanded respect with his ferocity and passion. The club was an amazing place that gave so many of us wonderful childhood memories. Coach Sheeler was as tough as they came, but he had a soft spot for coaching kids how to swim. He made us swim with shoes, shorts and t-shirts, something that I am sure would be illegal today. He not only made us better swimmers, but better people with great childhood memories.

Swimming became a family affair. My Dad wore the referee uniform of all white and walked the pool's edge watching us to make sure we swam correctly. He earned the nickname, "Eagle Eye" because he could always spot a mistake. If his hand went up as you were swimming, you were disqualified. Heck, he even disqualified me a few times. Not even I got special treatment! When he disqualified me the first time, I looked up at him in disbelief and said, "Couldn't someone else have done that instead of you?"

He cherished being a starter and firing the starter's pistol and enjoyed the camaraderie of the other referee dads. Dolly, with the patience of a saint, worked the clerk of courts corralling all us into the proper heats. I started swimming competitively in the six years old and under age group, and I still remember her getting us ready for our races.

One day I did not want to practice. I cried my eyes out so much I probably added an inch to the pool's water level. Coach Sheeler was on one side of the pool and Dolly on the other. I would swim twenty-five yards crying, and then hop out and start running. If I was on

Dolly's side, she would chase me down, pick me up and toss me back into the pool where I would, repeat the same to Coach Sheeler's side. Hop out, run, repeat. He would chase me down as I screamed and tossed me like a rainbow back into the pool. You would think I would tire them out at some point, but no, they didn't let me stop swimming.

Sheeler-Winton was such a magical place despite having to lift weights in a dark and damp weight room and sometimes swim with frogs. Coach Sheeler would have dances for the older kids, pancake breakfasts, and "Orange and Green" intra-squad meets. Which in retrospect, wasn't a good idea to load us up on pancakes then have us swim.

Coach Sheeler had an orange Corvette Stingray that he kept in mint condition and also a pick-up truck that had more rusted holes in it that I could count. When I got a bit older, around ten or eleven, I would hop on the side of the truck, as he drove through what seemed like a jungle, to dump the trash out behind the pool.

Sometimes during meets I would walk over to the department store called The Treasury and read comic books. This was at a time when an eight-year-old could just do that and not set off an Amber Alert. I don't even think my Dad or Dolly knew where I was, but I needed to get my Spider-Man fix!

When it got cold, by Miami standards, Dolly would stand by the edge of the pool with a towel in her outstretched hands. I would quickly hop out and she would wrap me up in her arms as we'd run to the warm car. She would have hot tea or hot chocolate waiting for me. I was lucky. I never saw any other parent doing that for their kids. They made them suffer in the cold.

In November of 1978, my paternal grandmother, Nana, passed away from cancer at age 62.

By the time I was eight, I had already lost my mother, my maternal grandparents and now my paternal grandmother. She was the one responsible for hiring Dolly, so her loss was huge. Despite this loss, her death was rarely talked about, as has been a pattern of my family. I did not attend her funeral in New York. Instead, I remained in Miami with my brother and Dolly. I did not really understand what her death meant, and I got no help from anyone either. My father shielded me from the pain of her death. The only thing I do remember was someone telling me, "Don't worry, one day you will see her again." Perhaps the adults just thought I was too young to understand, but even at my young age, I felt a void in my life without her. When my father returned from her funeral, life just continued for me as a kid.

Hanging out at the historic Parrot Jungle

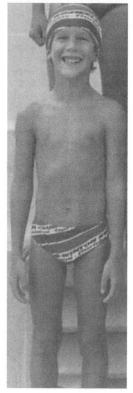

Chapter 9

Becoming Floridians

We were well on our way to becoming true Floridians. Right before I started third grade at Coral Reef Elementary, we finally moved into a four-bedroom ranch style house on 155th Terrace Street only a couple of miles from our old apartment. We now had our own pool. The garage was converted into a large family room with a storage room attached to it for the washer/dryer, toy chest and all of my dad's tools. My Dad was happy about that storage room.

Eventually we would have mangoes, orange, tangerine, banana, cherry and avocado trees. Dolly loved gardening. She made both a flower bed and a vegetable garden. Despite the four rooms, I still had to share one with Jeff. We didn't ask why; we just did what we were told. We took the bunk beds apart, but we're like the "Odd Couple." Jeff was messy and I was fairly neat on my side of the room. My Dad and Dolly were sharing the same room in the apartment so when we moved into the house, she had her own room where all her clothes were. By this time my father and her were a couple so at night they slept in my Dad's room. As I got older, my Dad slept in his recliner, like most father's across America and Dolly fell asleep on the couch. As a kid seeing them as a couple was normal, there was no, "Oh, so you two are a couple now?" type of thing, it was just a natural progression.

When they built a park next to the school, Dolly found a job in the main office. I would ride my bike to school, then head over to the park and do my homework until she was done with work at 3:30. I thought it was odd that I would ride my bike to school, then over to the park, and as Dolly drove home, I would have to ride back home too. Why not just throw my little dirt bike in the car? Nope.

My father was not a huge pet person, but we had fish. Let's be honest, they are not the most exciting pets to have. One day as Jeff and I got out of the car, we heard a chirping noise coming from inside the house. When we walked in, the chirping grew louder and I saw a gray cockatiel bird sitting in a cage by the window. The bird was about a foot long, from head to tail, with bright orange circles on the side of his head. His chirp was a high-pitched scream that almost sounded like "help!"

I was so excited to see the bird, but my father was a bit shocked. Dolly got me a bird, which made me a very happy boy. I named him Mickey after Mickey Mouse. What do you expect from a nine-year-old? The first time we took him out of the cage, we had to use yellow latex gloves because he bit so hard. Apparently, Dolly couldn't bring home a docile bird. She had to get the most violent one. But he was awesome and would eventually sit on my foot while I watched tv or fly through the house until he found me. He would sit on the back of my chair when I did homework, or he would climb up the curtain and sit, looking down at me. I think he was part dog because he always tracked me down no matter where I was in the house.

Over time we trained him or perhaps he trained us. Mickey quickly became part of the family, unlike the fish. He would jump out of his cage and walk to the table while we ate, sitting on my foot. I would put him on my shoulder and then he would walk down my arm and onto the table. Mickey would then go plate to plate and eat off it. I loved it, but my Dad hated it. Mickey would even mimic a sneeze or cough after hearing someone do it in the house.

He loved feet and he loved chirping at them. It was so weird, but funny. My bird had a foot fetish, but he didn't get it from me! He had a distinct personality that always made me smile despite his tendency to get territorial in some corners of the house. A couple of years later, my brother got a white cockatiel that he named Sunny, but she never talked or was as amusing as Mickey. Sunny came to our home after my brother's rabbit, Fluffy, died.

This home, our home, held so many incredible memories from birthday parties in our pool to celebrating Jewish holidays such as Passover Seders. Dolly learned how to cook Jewish food. It smelled so delicious as my great-grandmother and grandfather would lead us through the Seder. I couldn't focus on my part to read as my stomach growled in anticipation of eating. We would celebrate Hanukkah, and then Christmas for Dolly which was fun. I enjoyed seeing the tree lit up, but like most people, hated putting everything away when it was time to take the fake tree down.

My Dad taught me how to play catch in our yard and we would shoot water rockets up in the air that often landed on the roof. We had a huge poinsettia tree with a swing on it. In the summer, we would park the car underneath it for shade. Dolly would start dinner prior to picking us up from afternoon swim practice and when we walked into our home, it was filled with the amazing aroma of her cooking. We ate dinner as a family as we always waited for our father to get home from work. We would talk a bit, but we mostly watched games shows such as "Wheel of Fortune" or "Jeopardy!" throughout the years. Because I was the youngest, I had to sit with my back facing the television. But I usually got most of the answers right on Jeopardy, to the surprise of everyone else sitting at the table.

One memory that also stands out was about my mother. Dolly helped me tell someone about my mother for the first time. I was in elementary school and this memory is still burned into my brain as if it happened yesterday. Dolly was watching me and my neighbor swim and hang out on the patio. We were sitting along the side of the pool taking a break while Dolly sat at the table nearby. My neighbor looked around and asked, "Hey Michael, where is your mom?" This was the first time anyone asked me this question, so I was a bit stunned. Teachers never asked what happened to my mother after I wrote, "deceased" on those school information forms where it asked for mother's name. Did they even look at them? Now, here I was facing that five- hundred-pound gorilla and I couldn't just write "deceased" and leave it at that.

Feeling embarrassed and maybe even a little ashamed, I turned and looked at Dolly to see if she had heard him, but I couldn't tell if she did. I quickly responded, "I will tell you later," hoping he would forget about it and I could just avoid answering altogether. I was just a little kid, why did I have to answer such an adult question? However, Dolly did indeed hear this exchange between us and said, in her own strong and mothering voice, "Michael, it's okay, you can tell him now. Go ahead." I was so scared to say what happened out loud. My voice quivered with fear as my brain raced to try and find the words. I held my breath, looked at my friend, and said, "My mother is dead. She died in a car accident." I exhaled waiting for his response because I had no idea what he would say. He just simply said, "I'm sorry."

Just as Dolly knew when I was ready to walk all those years ago, she knew I was ready for this too. Even though I just told my friend about my mother, I was too young to really process what my mother's death meant and just continued being a kid.

My grandfather, Papa Ben, finally decided to leave the New York weather behind and also move to South Florida. He found a nice two - bedroom condo in North Miami Beach. My Aunt Sue lived with him for many years which was nice because we got to see her often too. My grandfather took me and Jeff to Biscayne Magic, a local magic store near him, and like most young boys, I was hooked. I was so fascinated by the man behind the counter. I couldn't get enough of the tricks he showed me. My mouth would be wide open, and I wouldn't blink, wondering how he did it. Naturally, I wanted to do what he was doing. I ended up getting one of those "starter magic kits" and it gave me many hours of enjoyment.

When I was ten, I started speech therapy, but my family had no idea if it was a lingering effect from my fractured skull or just a typical part of growing up. For a kid who couldn't say words that end in "ch" like "couch" or words beginning with "sh", magic gave me confidence to speak in front of others. I would practice for hours in my room, and then perform the tricks for my Dad and Dolly. During family functions, I would perform a show and loved making people laugh. I was in speech therapy for a couple of years and I can tell you this, I can say "shit" really good these days. Also, I want Sally who sold seashells by the sea shore to be eaten by a shark. I really despised Sally.

My father loved music and enjoyed Pete Fountain and Pavarotti. He once played the accordion and was a talented organ player. I remember him playing all the time, filling our house with music. I even took lessons for a while, and that made him proud. He often said, "Your long fingers are perfect for playing." I mostly liked hitting the drum button on the organ and all the other special effects more than playing, *You Light Up My Life*. Eventually I stopped with the lessons and focused on magic. My Dad seemed really happy playing the organ and it was heartbreaking many years later when it was damaged by Hurricane Andrew.

I had a pretty normal childhood made up of well...swimming. We didn't take family vacations because we had swim meets on what seemed like every weekend. I practiced magic, read Spider-man comics, Hardy Boys books, and listened to KISS. Jeff and I shared that room and KISS posters started appearing on "my side." I was pretty happy in my own little imaginative world.

Growing up I was very much into Star Wars and I wanted all the toys, from the movies, but toys cost money, and we were not rich. And just because I *wanted* the toys didn't mean I was necessarily going to *get* them. But maybe, I could *earn* them. After Empire Strikes Back came out in 1980, I developed a great positive reinforcement plan. It would not only help me become successful in the pool, but also would allow me to become my own Jedi Master. I used "The Force" when I approached my Dad and Dolly with this plan. A plan I thought was ingenious for a ten-year-old.

For each race, I had certain times I wanted to swim and a toy in mind that I wanted to earn. I asked them if I reached my goal times, would they agree to buy the toy.

Notice how I said *earned* and not *get* a toy. I figured it was only fair that I would earn a toy, right? I mean, I was swimming my butt off. There had to be more than a "good job" in it for me. There had to be STAR WARS!

I wrote down my goals on a little index card for the races I would swim in upcoming meets. The more time I took off, the bigger the toy. It made sense to me and more importantly to my Dad and Dolly. I do not know if they agreed just to shut me up, but I would like to think they saw me trying to set tangible goals in my young life. I think it made them proud that I came up with this plan. Surely, I could try to earn a medal, but the Millennium Falcon was so much better! Not to say medals and trophies are not wonderful tokens of your hard work, but I was ten when the plan went into action. I could not fly a trophy, but I could fly Luke's X-wing fighter! Teachable moment: Set your goals. Write them down on cards and make sure you have your reward set up.

I put a lot of pressure on myself to beat those times and earn those toys. Like many things in life, there were times when I worked my butt off and was .09 seconds short of my goal. I would be disappointed in myself. To work so hard and be that close. I think my parents recognized the hard work I put in and even though I failed to meet my overall goal, the fact I showed commitment and effort paid off with, maybe not the Star Wars toy I had in mind, but a different one.

It taught me the value of hard work when I put my mind to something. I can be lazy sometimes, but I can also work my butt off to make sure it is successful. If something does not go well, I know it's my fault and no one else's. If I missed the time by .09, it was not Dolly's fault—for not screaming loud enough or my coach's fault for not helping me enough. It was all mine. Something I think is surely missing in today's society is personal responsibility. Swimming taught me how to be responsible for my actions.

At Sheeler-Winton, we got to go to some really neat places. We even traveled to Jamaica and Nassau, the capital of the Bahamas, to swim against those teams. One of the coolest parts about traveling to Jamaica was that we got to visit Dolly's home in Maypen. From what I remember, it was a wooden home with no air conditioner and a large back yard where I would run around.

During our time in Nassau we stayed with a host family in their guest apartment. My teammate and I would slide down their stairs for hours of amusement. The teams also spent a lot of time at the beach playing in the sand and clear blue water. We would come home with ribbons and medals along with lifelong memories.

When I was twelve, Coach Sheeler decided to retire and close the swim club, which was quite sad. He built a ski lodge in Crested Butte, Colorado and wanted everyone to come out for ski lessons. For the last seven to eight years, the swim club was our second home. The club was like a family. We spent so much time together. The closing meant some of my teammates would swim for another team.

I can still remember my Dad and Dolly telling me the news. We were having one of our infamous breakfasts on the patio. I used to pick oranges from our orange tree and take them to the kitchen to make juice. The only problem was our juicer was so loud it would echo throughout the neighborhood as the smell of bacon floated through the air. As I returned to the table with the juice, my Dad said, "If you decide not to continue swimming, you will have to get a job. I don't care if it's flipping burgers, you will do something." That was always one of my Dad's favorite expressions, along with "I have a bone to pick with you."

Some of my teammates went to the Hurricanes Swim Club, that swam at the University of Miami, which was my first choice. According to my parents, "It was just too far" so we went to the Stingrays Swim Club at Miami Dade-Community College instead. Although we were leaving Sheeler-Winton, for a new chapter in our lives, it was the foundation of my youth, and I am sure the same for many of my fellow teammates.

I spent the next five years swimming for the Stingrays. I had a lot of swim coaches; some I liked; some I couldn't stand. I had one swim coach who eventually went on to become a Navy Seal. Once he left, his brother, a Vietnam Veteran, coached us. He was nice but smelled like cigarettes and always had his shirt unbuttoned most of the time. My Dad continued to serve as an official and Dolly worked the concession stand. She kept introducing more and more people to Jamaican meat pies which sold better than hamburgers. To this day, I have friends that remember those delicious pastries filled with meat and spices. The ones with the red mark on them were really spicy.

When I turned thirteen, like most Jewish kids, I had my Bar Mitzvah. Jeff had his at the house three years earlier. This was at a time where you could have a band play outside all night and into the morning and the neighborhood wouldn't care. We had covered the pool with plywood and put tables on them. We had an amazing party with the house packed with family and friends. When it came time for my Bar Mitzvah, we had it at a hotel on Key Biscayne with the typical cheesy Bar Mitzvah band. I had wanted KISS to perform which would have been awesome, but they never responded to my inquiries. Decades later in Indianapolis, at a KISS Expo, I told Paul Stanley this and he laughed. I am pretty sure all my friends who also had Bar Mitzvahs around the same time just re-gifted the exact same Polaroid camera.

I never paid attention in Hebrew school so my Bar Mitzvah instructor was not sure I would even make it to the big day. My reading and speaking of Hebrew was so poor. I had six months to get ready for the big day. This was not like reciting "Sally sold seashells down by the sea shore" either. He was so disappointed with me at first, but I practiced and learned my Hebrew just in time for me to become "an adult." It was one of the hardest things I ever had to do. This ordeal also made me realize that if I put my mind to something and work hard at it, I can be successful. Besides, I did not want to disappoint my father by not being prepared.

Speaking of being prepared, I was quite unprepared the first time I encountered a situation where Dolly's skin color was an issue. It happened in, of all places, at Hebrew School. Yes, Hebrew School! As we waited to be picked up, we stood outside the building. Parents would drive down the driveway and then loop around to pick us up. One day I was standing there with a fellow classmate waiting for Dolly. As she looped around and came within view of my classmate, he saw her and said, "Hey, I didn't know your mother was a nigger." This was the first time someone ever said something like that to me. I knew the word was especially derogatory towards black people, but hearing it directed to me, and towards Dolly was a first and quite shocking.

With the word still lingering in the air, I turned towards him and nearly pushed him through the stained-glass window of the classroom behind us and said, "Don't you ever say that again! That's my mother!" By then the car was right there and I hopped in. As Dolly drove away she asked me what happened. I didn't know what to say and just said that he said something stupid that I did not like. I did not want to hurt her feelings and mention a word that means something so horrible to her. Above all, he said it about Dolly and just as she defended me, I had to stand up and defend her. I am also sure if I had told her, she would have jammed on the brakes and went back for him. He was definitely not invited to my Bar Mitzvah.

Back to my Bar Mitzvah. It had a "swimming theme" and my Dad took countless rolls of film of me swimming, of me in my swimsuit and of me with my medals and trophies. He was a photographer in his younger days, and he really got into it. I was not a natural model with my braces and mop hair, but we finally found the right picture for a mock up cover of *Swimming World* magazine. I wrote my very first speech and my father wrote "slow down" in huge letters in the margins, since sometimes I would speak too fast or mumble. Funny how I remember that when I give a speech or perform comedy today because sometimes, I still speak too fast.

I know my parents paid a lot for the photographer, but I eventually got tired of smiling on command. It stinks to look back at some of the pictures because I look so unhappy since I could not smile in all one thousand photos. The swimming theme was perfect, and many of my teammates who were my friends attended the event. Swimming fostered so many great memories.

In 9th grade, the Stingrays went to Europe to represent the United States along with the Fort Lauderdale swim team. We were a bunch of Florida kids traveling to Germany, Austria and Switzerland, in January. Seeing snow again was fantastic, as I barely remembered it from New York. We had so much fun, but I swam so badly because I was extremely nervous. I ended up getting the flu prior to coming back, so that ruined the return trip for me. But at least I slept the whole way back on the flight. I also had the honor of swimming in the Junior Maccabi Games for Jewish athletes in Detroit and Toronto.

Back in the States, our team worked at the Orange Bowl concession stand to raise money for the trip to Europe. Seeing the Miami Hurricanes and Miami Dolphins play while working was an amazing experience. Dan Marino was in his second year in 1984 and I remember getting his autograph while holding his Miller Lite. The concession stand itself was horrific and if you were a germaphobe and OCD you'd need to be hosed down before and after every game. I never felt so grimy in my entire life. I worked the cash register with Dolly, and she taught me how to count up for making change. This was back in the 80's so we didn't have fancy digital registers like now. I was also in charge of the soda tanks and for some reason the CO_2 would always go out during half time. The tank weighed more than I did. Why a fourteen-year-old was in charge of that beats me. But there is nothing like thirsty fans in the south Florida heat waiting for their drinks.

Another fond memory I recall, was seeing the Jackson Victory Tour where everyone dressed like Michael Jackson. I also saw Prince's Purple Rain concert. I was not a fan of these artists but there is no denying these shows were historic. Life as a teenager was pretty fun with swimming and watching the games in the Orange Bowl. I was looking forward to high school and seeing what would be next in my life. Jeff graduated high school in 1985 and earned a swimming scholarship to LaSalle University in Philadelphia. For the first time, I would finally have my own tidy room.

Happy Father time at my Bar Mitzvah, June 4th, 1983

During many photoshoots with my Dad for
my Bar Mitzvah.

Chapter 10

Lessons from Wearing a Speedo

The doctors that treated me, along with my family, had no idea how or *if* I would recover fully from the crash. No one knew if I would have a normal life, but yet, somehow, I healed. I'd like to say it was my strong will to live, but I was only an infant, so I doubt my determination had anything to do with it. Perhaps infants are just more resilient than adults when it comes to injuries because we don't know any better or really, anything at all.

I learned a lot about life from swimming—not just how to shave my legs! I could not have been successful in the water, or in life, without my coaches. Some of them I really liked. Some I hated. But they all pushed me to become better. If you want to accomplish goals, you always need help even when you think you are all alone. I remember swimming the mile and thinking, *Well, it's just you in this pool swimming all these laps. No one else is going to help you.* No one is going to hop in and swim for you. It was nice to see your coach on the side of the pool yelling at you to go faster while gesturing something else. No, NOT that gesture. It would be a gesture that I was on pace or that I needed to speed it up. Not one person in this world has accomplished anything without help. Even on the days when I think I am completely alone; I have to remember there is assistance.

Swimming was not just a sport; it was a way of life. It helped keep me out of trouble and away from drugs. Although I may have been yelled at plenty of times during practice, it was a healthy way to grow up. All that yelling gave me tough skin. Swimming taught me about goal setting, positive reinforcement and the will to succeed. Nowadays if someone tells me I can't do it, I will try my hardest to prove them wrong. That sense of accomplishment feels so satisfying.

Throughout my life, I have been told that I do not take the time to enjoy my accomplishments, as I should. I accomplish one thing and am already on the next goal, because in swimming once I earned a personal best time, it was like, *okay, now, could you swim faster?* Must be the competitor in me.

Swimming taught me how to work with others in groups, even when you really don't want to. Sometimes you will have ten people in a lane, with only five seconds in between each other when you push off the wall. You swim down the right side of the lane, do a turn and come back on the opposite side. That is circle swimming. When you start doing this type of "group activity", you learn pretty quickly how to work with others because someone has to go first, second, third and so on. You have to pay attention because if you don't, you could get kicked in the face if you are too close to the person in front of you.

It is difficult to achieve success by yourself and in swimming; I had coaches and teammates to help stay motivated. In school, it was my teachers—well, some of them anyway. In comedy, in a warped way, other comedians keep you motivated by enthusiastically saying "you suck," when a joke bombs. If the method works, why change it? Especially when it was all done from the heart. Friends are great to have around for support because even if you are competing against each other, someone has to win, so why not a friend? Yes, there may be jealousy if my friend wins, but that only gives me more motivation to be better next time. I've noticed that the competitiveness I've learned in swimming carried over to comedy. If my friend was on stage before me getting laughs, I wanted to get more laughs than he or she. There is nothing wrong with wanting to be the best at what you do. Never feel bad about that. If I goofed off in the pool, classroom, or stage, then the results demonstrated those decisions. Teamwork will help you become better. When the whole team swims well, you win. When all the comedians on stage do well, the audience walks out happy.

Another valuable lesson I learned from swimming is about preparation. Tie your swimsuit before getting on the blocks! Look, if you're a swimmer and you don't have your suit tied and you're about to swim the mile, it's going to be an unforgettable race that will haunt you as soon as you dive into that pool. The suit comes right off. Just make sure you are prepared in life; nothing could be worse than training for something and then have it all derailed by not "tying your suit." For example, if you are presenting a program, you do not want all that hard work to go to waste at the last minute because you overlooked one small detail.

As a student, you have to be prepared for tests. I remember studying poetry in English class. I loathe poetry. I cannot figure out the meaning, the syntax, any of it. I did not read the assignments so when the test came, my suit was totally untied. I wrote my name on the paper, looked at the questions and could not answer a single one. I turned in the blank paper and left the class. I learned a very valuable lesson after that. No, not to enjoy poetry, but my professor said, if you did not understand it, ask for help. He would have taken the time to work with me. Just like when I was younger and could not tie my swimsuit, my Dad or Dolly did it until I could. It taught me to ask for assistance, even though, at times, I still don't, I just jump right in without my suit being tied.

Along with your suit not being tied, there is so much going through your mind before the race. If a swimmer is not prepared mentally, then the race is already lost. Once you are on those blocks, you are focused on the start. Then you fly through the air and everything else is automatic. You've been training for that race. You know what you are doing until you dive in and your goggles come off - now what? Can't just stop, pick your head up and fix them, although, I have seen many swimmers do that, including myself when I was younger. When I was a kid, I did not have the mental ability to just continue without them.

In life, your goggles may come off and one side fills up with water, how will you adapt? Swimming taught me the mental toughness to continue with one side filled up and swim the best race I can, even if I can only see with one eye. Or you rip the goggles off in that moment and get swimming. How mentally prepared are you to adjust on the fly like that?

It can happen a lot in comedy when you're on stage and a joke bombs. You have a split second to adjust in front of an audience and trust me, they will smell that fear coming from you. Sometimes I still freak out a bit internally when things do not go as planned. It is probably because I envision something, as if I did before a race, and see it perfectly. But when something goes astray, I may lose focus or my mind temporarily. And sometimes I have people around me that help me through it, which is nice.

We learned in swimming to visualize our races as a form of mental preparation. We would lie on the pool deck on thin towels, because that screams comfort when you want to focus on something so important like a race. We would relax and do some sort of deep breathing that has you starting with "in through the nose and out through the mouth." The only problem was I had a severe deviated septum, so breathing through the nose was nearly impossible.

Years later when I had it fixed, the doctor said my nose was worse than the guy who was punched in the nose with brass knuckles. I was in my early thirties when I was finally able to breathe normally. That septum gave me a lot of trouble. I would have to take a deep breath in order to even kiss a girl, but I digress. Back to mental prep. We would relax and visualize our race, from start to finish including all the minute details of the race. Turns out I used mental prep in school too, but my teachers often called it daydreaming.

Visualizing your goals is especially important. Dream about it, focus on it. What does it feel like to you? Do you visualize being debt free? What does it feel like to you? Visualize seeing that balance on those credit cards reach zero how does that feel? I still envision it. What about weight loss? It is just a matter of relaxing the body with some deep, slow breaths so you are relaxed and focus the mind on what you want to achieve. I have a hyperactive imagination and I also use it when I write a new joke. I see the audience laughing which in reality is not always the case. The reality could be that you only hear your fellow comedians in the back of the room laughing which is not the "visualized result!" If only your comedian friends are laughing and the audience is not, it is a long walk back from the stage, because they're laughing AT you, not WITH you. But we've all felt that pain leaving the stage. We stay motivated to get back up on stage as soon as possible.

The last thing I learned from my days as a swimmer is a lesson from Pete Leighton who was one of my many swim coaches. Pete coached me at the Stingray Swim Club when I was in high school. Sadly, he passed away years ago, but I never forgot his lesson about choices and consequences in life. In between sets, I said, "Hey Pete, I have to go to the bathroom." He said, "No you don't." In which I replied, "Yes, yes I do." He countered with, "No, you don't, you don't have to get out." I responded with, "Yes, I have to get out and go, now." Then he laid this gem on me with his smile, "You don't have to do anything in life but die." Being the smart-ass teen that I thought I was, with a full bladder, I would challenge him on this incredulous false statement.

"What about paying taxes? You have to pay those. You have to pay rent. You have to eat," I said defiantly. He cocked his head to the side, smiled again, and replied, "You don't have to pay your taxes or pay your rent or even eat." He was right. You choose to do those things. If you don't do those things, there are consequences, but you don't HAVE to do them. It reminded me of my father telling me after I complained about a teacher giving me a bad grade. His response was, "She only recorded the grade you earned." Pete's statement of, "The only thing you have to do in life is die," is still burned into my memory. It is such a simple statement, but yet so powerful. If we choose something good or bad, there are always consequences. But I know what you are really thinking; did I get out to use the bathroom? Yes, yes, I did and then I had an extra set to do. I made a choice and I suffered the consequences. Thanks Pete!

I had another coach named Peter Prinz who reminded me of Coach Sheeler in a way, because he had a tough exterior, but such a big heart, and he pushed us to be better. He would walk up and down on the side of the pool yelling or whistling at us throughout the practice. Sometimes he would throw pull buoys or kickboards at us. He graduated from the University of Florida, so it was fun to trash talk with him when the Gators played Miami. He could sense when I wasn't giving him my full potential and while it may have been "tough love," his pushing helped me to be better. In my current role as an academic adviser at Kent State University, I sometimes treat my students like Coach Peter, just without throwing kickboards at their heads. I push them to be successful.

All those years swimming and I learned so many life lessons from just wearing a Speedo. When you are a kid and swimming, you are just caught up in the moment. One practice to the next, one meet to the next, one Speedo to, well, you get the idea. I feel an athlete should be able to take life lessons from their sport. I tell football players that homework is like watching game tapes and their tests are the game.

We did not have "participation trophies" when I swam. If you came in first, second or third, you got a medal or trophy. Fourth through Eighth? You get to practice harder for next time. Not only did I learn about competition and responsibility, but also about setting goals and more importantly, achieving those goals. I still use what I learned from the pool, just not in a Speedo - no one needs to see that!

Chapter 11

Dr. Magic

In addition to school and swimming, I continued with magic and even joined the International Brotherhood of Magicians when I was fifteen. My Dad would drive me to the meetings held at Ponce De Leon High School near the University of Miami. Sometimes I think my father was more into magic than I was. Perhaps he was living vicariously through me or maybe he just enjoyed watching me perform. He was my biggest supporter and would drive me to every meeting. We weren't rich by any means and a lot of tricks were expensive to buy.

Harry Anderson was one of my first influences in magic. I was drawn to the way he blended magic with comedy. When Harry was on the Tonight Show my Dad would let me stay up to watch him. Many years later I had the opportunity to be Harry's opening act in Cleveland. It was wonderful to not only watch him perform live, but to also thank him for being such an influence on my career. And like any "fanboy" asked him to sign his books for me, and a picture with him, which he did.

My first stage name was "Magical Michael." Yeah, I know, not the most creative, but I was in my early teens, what do you expect? I was a true professional because I had business cards! Our magic club would go see David Copperfield when he came to town. We got to meet him for autographs and a group picture. When my great-grandmother, Sophie told me, "You will grow up and be a doctor," I didn't want to disappoint her. Sadly, there was no way I was smart enough to be a doctor, so I changed my stage name to "Dr. Magic." Oh, I still have the brochures of me in a tuxedo looking just like every other magician out there.

My father would pressure me to bring a trick along when we went out with friends for dinner. I hated that because I respected the stage and never wanted to force a trick on people. Sometimes I felt like a trained monkey, with magic. But I discovered I was good at comedy and magic, so I enjoyed performing for people's birthday parties. I think I may have done an act for every Joey who turned four one summer! Before I had my driver's license, my father would drop me off at the birthday party house and then pick me up when I was done. When we couldn't afford the two-hundred-dollar shiny magic case in the store, we went to Home Depot and built our own with sixty bucks worth of wood. I still have it in my garage with tricks that I cannot remember how to do. Then, when I was seventeen, I won 2nd place in the close-up and stage contests at the Florida State Magic Convention.

During my days at Miami Palmetto High School, I had friends in classes, but I always felt alone during lunch as a lot of them would leave campus to eat. Dolly would make our lunches which was WAY better than what Miami-Dade Public Schools provided for us, but I never wanted to sit in the cafeteria. So, I would sit in the hallway eating alone or with a teacher I knew who also swam at Miami-Dade Community College. I didn't have her for class, I just knew her from swimming, so it was nice to have lunch with a friend.

As I was starting my junior year, I experienced a life altering event that set me on the path of actually doing *The Magic of Life*. One day my father asked me to get his wallet out of his dresser. As I opened the drawer, I noticed a yellowish piece of paper. It was an old article about the crash. I turned it over in my hands and began to read words about that event that took my mother from us. As I read it, I realized I didn't recall my father telling me it was a drunk driving crash that had altered my entire life. He held onto this for fifteen years. How many times did he read it? Did he relive the crash each time he read it? I am sure he didn't need this piece of paper as a reminder. Reading that hit me deep in my soul. My father never talked about it much. Seeing the words in print were powerful. My mother's death wasn't an accident, she was a victim of a crime.

There was something inside of me, upon knowing it was a drunk driver, that made me want to do something. I could not let my mother's death, and almost mine, be for nothing. I felt rage and anger for the first time regarding my mother's death. Either I could do something to make a difference or I could do nothing. I had no idea how I would carry through with it, just that I needed to.

I decided to get involved with Students Against Drunk Driving (SADD), as it was called back then. We had a small group of peers. We even put together a presentation for the junior high school about drugs. I grew up in Miami during the years of Miami Vice, 2 riots,

Scarface and the "glorious" drug days. I used my magic skills to come up with something creative that was centered around drugs. It was pretty fun writing a new "patter" for the tricks rather than what I learned when I first bought them.

I continued to day dream my way through most classes but excelled in communications and writing. I hated math and science with a passion. I would have anxiety the second I turned on that Texas Instrument calculator. But I found joy outside the classroom. A turning point in my life was going to Coconuts Comedy Club in North Miami Beach near my grandfather. As soon as I saw people's names and pictures on the table tents, I thought, *this is what I want to do in life.* I bought Judy Brown's *Stand-up Comedy: The Book and* learned how to write jokes. I started to write observations about life in a notebook and practiced stand-up in my speech class during my senior year. A love affair was growing inside me. Comedy felt right. I knew it was what I wanted to do with my life. Harry Anderson gets a lot of credit for being one of my influences, but at the time I was also getting into Robin Williams, Seinfeld, Jay Leno and watched

Johnny Carson's monologue even though my parents thought I was asleep.

Growing up as a KISS fan, I never had the opportunity to see the original band. My room was like a KISS shrine with all their posters. I bought my first ticket to their *Crazy Nights* concert in 1988 when I was seventeen. I had my driver's license, but my Dad and Dolly would not let me drive my friend Larry and I to the Hollywood Sportatorium. I was a little disappointed since I was already driving to swim practice, but they said they would drive us instead. I borrowed my grandfather's disc camera and snuck it into the concert to capture the incredible occasion. I had chills throughout the entire concert as I sang each song loud and proud. I was in KISS heaven. As the show ended, I came crashing back to earth. ninety minutes of bliss made me want more. I haven't missed a tour since.

After I graduated from high school, I lived out my lifelong dream of doing stand-up comedy at Uncle Funny's Comedy Club in Miami. Up until this time, the magic tricks helped get the laughs, but now I wanted to see if the material I wrote was any good. It was the most nerve-wracking thing I ever had to do. My Bar Mitzvah speech was a walk in the park compared to this. I was as nervous as I have ever been in my life. I didn't want my Dad or Dolly there in case I was horrible and embarrassed myself; and them too.

As I sat in one of the booths with the feature act that night, I could tell he picked up on my nervousness. "Are you nervous?" he asked me with a smile. "Hell yes I am! I've been performing magic the last few years, but never stand-up comedy," I responded enthusiastically. "It's just physical energy, you'll be fine once you get on stage."

As nice as that seemed, tell that to my churning stomach. That comedian's name was Scott Thompson, but you may know him better as Carrot Top. In terms of my set, I might have gotten two laughs as I rushed my set because I was so scared. I wish I had remembered my Dad's advice for my Bar Mitzvah speech: slow down. I went back to Uncle Funny's one more time before leaving for college, putting my dream of being a comedian on hold. Even if I never stepped foot on the stage again, I fulfilled my dream in comedy and that is what mattered the most to me.

Chapter 12

Hello Ohio, Goodbye Sunshine

In April 1988, during my senior year spring break, I went on a recruiting trip to Ashland College (now University) in Ashland, Ohio. Go ahead and Google it, because I had no idea where it was either. If you've never been in Ohio during April, trust me, you can experience all four seasons in the same day. I knew little about the college. Back then we couldn't just research schools online.

What I did know, is I wanted to see what was outside the sunshine state. I had only lived in two states and hardly remembered New York. I wanted a change of scenery. Growing up, it felt like my father was sometimes overprotective of me—I guess you couldn't blame him— but I wanted to leave home. I wanted some breathing room and felt like I needed to discover who I really was.

My recruiting trip got off to an interesting start. As I stepped off the plane in sunny Cleveland the coach greeted me and said, "Hi Michael, are you ready to party?" I may have had a few beers from time to time, but I had never been drunk before. I was fairly good combating high school peer pressure when it came to alcohol and drugs, but right off the bat I felt pressured by him to drink. I wanted to fit in and make a good impression. This made me think of the time when Jeff came back from his first recruiting trip. On the way home from the airport our father asked him, "So, how many beers did you drink?" Oddly enough, my Dad wouldn't ask me that when I returned home from this particular trip.

I remember the scenery in the car as we made small talk for the hour or so drive to Ashland. I saw farms, cows, and open land. I didn't see the malls, traffic and bad drivers that I was accustomed to in Miami. I still recall seeing this farm on I-71 South on the eastern side of the highway with silos and a barn. I knew I was in a different world. I was used to passing a Burger King and McDonalds on nearly every corner in Miami. When we got off the exit on Route 250, I saw nothing but land. On one side of the highway was Grandpa's Cheesebarn and on the other, a truck stop. It was refreshing and intriguing to see such a different environment.

As we drove into town, I thought, "What do people do here for work and for fun?" There was a sign that read, *future site of Burger King* on a piece of land across the street from the pool. What do you mean, FUTURE? I was stunned! This town had no Burger King yet? I felt like Marty McFly going back in time. I could already see Ashland was such a small town, I didn't know how this was going to go.

I was quickly subjected to the Ohio weather as the sun disappeared and the temperature dropped. It started to rain. I met a swimmer named Matt who was going to be my host during my stay. He lived in a large room called a "triple" in Kilhefner Hall with two other swimmers. Kilhefner Hall was a musty, old building that had a lot of history in it. His room was dark and drab. It matched the weather outside. It rained most of my trip.

I met another recruit, Bryan, from Nashville, who stayed with other swimmers on a different floor. Bryan had blonde hair, was about my height, wore cowboy boots, and had southern accent. We had one single thing in common: we both swam distance freestyle and breaststroke. But we seemed to hit it off. We made our way across the street to the athletic building which housed the gym, a small weight room and pool. It was our turn to "showcase" our abilities for the coach by swimming a little bit and meet the rest of the small team.

The indoor pool was nothing I've ever seen before. I was used to huge outdoor pools in Miami. This was a glorified bath tub. The wretched smell of chlorine burned my nostrils. The water was cloudy. Instead of the eight lanes that I was used to, this only had six. The walls had soundproofing panels with the letter "A" painted in purple on them. The swimming program was nonexistent for some years and it was just resuscitated the year prior, so the team had no more than 20 people.

While on the trip, I got to meet with an advisor about the courses I would be taking. Then I met the director of the theater department. I never acted a day in my life, but I thought, with the magic I was performing, why not go into theater with zero acting experience? Makes great sense, right? When he said, "Would you like to walk out on stage?" I wasn't even thinking about acting in a play. I thought how cool it would be to perform magic or comedy in front of 700 people. What did I know about acting? I daydreamed of being on Carson, not Broadway. I even thought about film school too.

Then came the drinking. So much drinking. As I said before, I rarely drank, but I felt the peer pressure to fit in among the other swimmers on this trip. I wanted to be liked and be a part of their group. I already felt like a stranger, being from Miami, so I caved and drank with them. It was the first time I experienced a hangover and boy did that suck. But hey, at least I was making friends, right? If that was the worst thing to happen, I knew I would be just fine.

Except for a moment, I was not. What happened with the coach the next day felt worse than the hangover. I was sitting in the coach's office. We were discussing swimming and my scholarship. As I sat across from him at his desk, smelling like chlorine, I didn't know what to expect from this conversation. It was my first ever recruiting trip.

He surveyed a paper on his desk. Little did I know; he wrote a certain dollar amount pertaining to my scholarship. As we're talking, I looked down at his sheet and saw he crossed out that amount and wrote a lesser amount on the paper. That's right, he changed my scholarship right before me and didn't even say a word about it. As a seventeen-year-old, I simply thought that was odd and that it wasn't my place to question it. I didn't have my father there to give me advice or advocate for me, so I remained quiet.

I was too afraid to say anything, but I knew it was wrong. I was just happy that I would be earning a scholarship. Not bad for a kid who seventeen years earlier doctors had no idea if I would ever be normal. This wasn't just for me, but also for my Dad and Dolly and all they put into swimming for me. I wanted them to be proud of me. Ashland was by far the most different place I had experienced. I had written to other schools but hadn't visited them yet. Heck, I didn't even know if we could afford any other visits. I had nothing to compare Ashland to either but despite my original misgivings about the place, something about it felt right. It's almost like when you meet someone on a first date and there is a spark. It's like, why even bother going out with other people?

I wanted to leave home and Ashland seemed like a good fit for me. Jeff went to LaSalle in Philadelphia and I was going to attend a school in rural Ohio with a

Brethren affiliation. Great place for a good Jewish boy who was raised by a Jamaican woman.

I was nervous, but confident, as I was about to start my freshman year. I was supposed to be rooming with a football player, but he dropped out before school even started. The school asked if I would be okay rooming with a student from Haiti and I thought, "Why wouldn't I be?" I thought it was an odd question. Dolly was proud of me for earning a scholarship and excited about my new adventure in life. I was definitely going to miss her and her home cooking.

My Dad and I flew up together and he drove to campus for orientation week. He enjoyed playing tourist as he drove which made me nuts because he was driving so slowly. At one restaurant in Mansfield, we had a nice laugh. The waitress asked us, "What type of pop do you want?" My father remembered pop from growing up in New York, but in Miami, we called everything "coke." I was finding Ohio to be quite different than South Florida in every way imaginable.

My father and I ended up having dinner with Coach. That evening my entire perspective changed.

Coach apologized for his wife's absence by sarcastically saying, "Her boss is Jewish and wouldn't let her out of work early." Wait...what?! Changing my scholarship was one thing, but this was entirely different. It still makes me mad when I think about it. It was the first time I heard such a remark about Jews.

I was waiting for my Dad to say something, but since he either didn't hear it or chose to ignore it, I didn't say anything either. If that would happen today, I wouldn't hesitate to say something. But back then I just kept my mouth shut. It was hurtful yet confusing at the same time. Coach didn't know I was Jewish at the time either, but it should not have mattered. Little did I know it was just the start of many anti-Semitic experiences I would be faced with at college.

Bryan, whom I met on my recruiting trip, ended up living a few doors down from me. Two other swimmers and a wrestler lived across from me in a triple. This was great because I met them on my recruiting trip. My Dad hovered as I put my things in my room. I was ready for him to go home so I could start the next chapter of my life. He may not have been ready to cut the cord, but I was. Like a typical college student, I would still call him for money, care packages of hot chocolate and Chef Boyardee, while sharing updates on how college was going on a weekly basis.

My new life was pretty much swimming, classes and watching people play a card game called Euchre. No one would teach me how to play which was fine because I was focused on adjusting to the homework in college. With all the papers I had to type I was thrilled that I was forced to take a typing class in high school. The team was required to do study tables in the library after dinner. I was so tired after practice. I usually fell asleep in my cubicle instead of reading history or psychology. Except one time when I assisted in getting the swim team kicked out of study tables for a week or so in the library because we tossed around a football. It was better than falling asleep in my cubicle.

I remember in my freshman orientation class we had to write a paper that answered three questions, "Who am I?" "Where did I come from?" and "Where am I going?" I wish I kept that paper to see what my eighteen-year-old self-wrote and how much of it came true. I was entering college with a blank canvas. It was nice. That canvas would be a fresh start with the independence of being away from home. I would soon discover who I was in life. I still called home on Sundays, but now I had to make my own decisions in life. My father and Dolly were the sounding board, but at the end of the day, the decisions were mine to make. Good, Bad or Ugly.

We had swim practice at 5:30 a.m. Despite showering after swimming, I just couldn't get that chlorine off my body and it itched. If I could smell it on me I wonder what my classmates smelled when I sat next to them. Our weight room that year was, in what seemed like, a janitor's closet in the gym behind one of the basketball nets. The Ashland weight machines made Sheeler-Winton's gym seemed state-of-the-art.

Our team also had walk-ons like one guy named Sean from Columbus. Sean didn't have a typical swimmer's build as he was a bit stocky. If he ever did shave down for swimming, it would take a lot of razors because he looked like Chewbacca. After practice I saw him sitting by himself eating dinner in our cafeteria known as "Convo." I walked over to him and said, "Hey, swimmers sit over there," pointing to where the team was eating. I grabbed his swim bag as he followed me over to our tables. Although he wasn't the fastest guy, he put in a lot of effort. Throughout the year, me, Sean and Bryan became close friends. Bryan and I swam in the same lane since we were distance swimmers. When you spend that much time with someone, you're going to become friends.

Before I knew it, it was October and Homecoming was upon us. I was thrilled to learn that Jerry Seinfeld was coming. I watched his HBO Special many times. He was a major comedic influence. I remember watching him during his performance and thought, *that is what I want to do one day*. Seeing KISS was one thing, but after doing magic for so long and my two attempts at stand-up comedy, it was still a goal of mine to perform. I don't know when or where it was going to happen but seeing Seinfeld for the first time made me feel what musicians must feel when they saw the Beatles or KISS for the first time.

Our swimming season started in October and ran through February. During one of our meets at the University of Findlay, we met a recruit, a red headed guy named Dennis from New Jersey. He was a fellow breastroker and seemed liked a good guy. Dennis had a memorable introduction to the team. One day, during a diving event, he ended up burping really loud. It echoed throughout the indoor pool. He was standing behind us and the entire team slowly turned and looked at him. Later that day, we thought we lost him. Turns out he went walking around town. We spotted him coming back from Big Lots, the proud owner of a Bon Jovi cassette.

During my first semester, my classes were going well, and I was excited about one of my assignments in Introduction to Theater. We were asked to write a play, which I was very eager to do. I knew I wasn't cut out to act, but I enjoyed working behind the scenes and writing. I switched my major to communications which prompted a meeting with my swim coach. I told him, "Swimming would just interfere with any plays, and I like communications a lot better, it suits me."

The play I wrote for the assignment dated December 14th, 1988 is called, "Hi Mom, It's Me Your Son," which is, you guessed it, autobiographical. It was about me going to visit my mom's grave for the first time.

My Dad never took us or even suggested it growing up, so I had to use my imagination like I had been doing throughout my life.

I'm not a hoarder but I am glad I kept this play from college to look back on. I think the fact it was one-sided, from my perspective, is what bothered me the most. I still long for that "Good job son" or "I love you son" from her. People say she would be proud of me but hearing the words from her will never happen and that still torments me.

I wrote, "This play is about a boy who has a difficult time understanding the reasons why his mother died. He confronts this problem with his father." My professor gave me an A minus and said, "Nice blend of humor and pathos."

I learned that after swimming season came "drinking season," which started in February after our championship meet at Cleveland State University. I didn't drink my first semester and my GPA was over 3.0. Before we left Cleveland to head back to campus, someone was taking orders for what we wanted to drink. Again, the peer pressure to partake was enormous. I didn't want to be left out, so I said, "How about some rum?" I had a rum and Coke, courtesy of Dolly, back at my Bar Mitzvah, so I thought, why not now?

The party took place in my teammates' room across the hall where Coach would duck into the closet every time someone knocked on the door. I am not sure the ratio between rum and coke, but I ended up on the bathroom floor hugging the toilet bowl that night. Coach would also have parties at his house which continued into next year too. What is one to do when there is all that pressure on you to be part of the team both inside the pool and out? I fell into the typical college lifestyle during my second semester and my GPA slipped below 3.0.

As Sean and I bonded during our freshman year, we decided to become roommates for our sophomore year. Sean and I had a lot in common. I was four days older, and Sean's father passed away when he was a toddler. We also shared the pain of going to the mail room where our mailboxes were right to each other only to hear the worker yell "EMPTY!" the majority of the time. We were two goofballs who thought living together would be perfect. I decided to move down to the opposite side of the floor, along with other swimmers. I think we were just trying to make a "swimming wing." With freshman year coming to a close, I was looking forward to returning to Miami for a nice break.

Chapter 13

The Six-Pack

As I happily returned to Ashland for my sophomore year, I was anxious to see what it would bring. Living on a different side of the floor meant meeting new people too. Across from Sean and I, was a freshman football kicker, Brent, from Delphos, Ohio. Funny story. Sean was introduced to Brent's mom in an awfully unique way. A nice Jewish boy, who will remain nameless, took Sean's towel from the showers forcing him to walk back to his room naked as the day he was born. As he tried to get into our locked room, the door to Brent's room opened and his mom emerged. Their eyes met for a brief second, but not before Brent's mom had to quickly avert eyes after seeing Sean, who quickly smiled and said, "Hi, Brent's mom!"

Next to Brent, was John Kelly, another freshman from Lakewood, Ohio. John stood 6'5", weighed around two hundred and eighty pounds and played offensive line in high school. He quickly earned the nickname "Big John" by everyone who lived on the 2nd floor of Kilhefner Hall and soon the entire university. John was an amazingly gentle giant with a caring and outgoing personality. He would do anything for anyone, including giving you the shirt off his enormous back.

John was a *very* heavy sleeper. Sometimes he would never hear his alarm blasting away. So much so that on occasion, when I would return from morning practice, I would go into his room and turn off his alarm, so I could go back to sleep. I would see him later on in the day perplexed as to how he missed class. And, Dennis, that redhead burper who stopped an entire diving event with his memorable sound, also arrived on campus that year. Dennis lived in a different dorm, but we were glad to have him on campus.

It's pretty amazing when you can look back and pinpoint exactly when you became best friends with certain people. The six of us all came from different backgrounds and yet quickly became brothers. On the weekends if Brent didn't have a game or we didn't have a swim meet, we would hang out together and watch movies or WWF. We were six goofballs that enjoyed having fun. It was all that mattered.

Unlike my first semester, I drank a little during swimming season. Coach still had parties at his house, so it was just the culture. Ashland became a "dry" campus my sophomore year, but there was more alcohol on campus than the previous one because now it was a challenge to sneak it in. Alcohol was just part of our lives now and yes; it impacted my grades. The thing is, when you're having parties at your coach's house or while you're snowed in at Buffalo and the entire team is drinking, you continue to lose sight of who you are due to peer pressure. No one twisted my arm, but yet, I still felt the need to fit in with everyone.

I understood I came from an exceptionally different and diverse background compared to everyone I met in Ashland. But I was still dumbfounded when I heard racist remarks. Was this how people really felt? We all busted on each other, but it still bothered me. My peers were quick to utter anti-Semitic and racist remarks. One time at coach's house, while watching Notre Dame play, he told me why he didn't like the University of Miami football team. "I don't like them because they are a bunch of niggers," Coach said. I was so stunned I didn't know what to say. It was just like we were back in the restaurant with my father. I told him that it wasn't true. I wish I had the strength to tell him exactly what I wanted to say, but I didn't and felt that I failed Dolly in that moment.

I used my humor to deflect all comments coming my way. I lost count of all the "Jew" jokes I would hear. The way I saw it, they never met a Jew before, so I had to educate them about what they thought they knew. I was called "Jesus Killer" by people who said they were "only joking." I didn't believe them. So, I fought fire with humor. As much as it hurt, I could not let them see how much pain it was causing me. If they knew, I figured they would just do it more and more. I would get all the typical Jewish stereotype comments and sometimes they would just pile on. During my freshman year one guy on my floor called me "Toucan" after "Toucan Sam" from the Fruit Loops cereal box due to my "Jewish nose." It hurt, and I hated it, but I deflected it with humor by putting Toucan Sam onto my door. No one was going to stick up for me. By putting it on my door I felt that I took away his power over me. I figured if I did that it would eventually come from a place of teasing, instead of hatred.

When they would throw a quarter on the ground and say, "Hey Jew, look a quarter," I would pick it up because if they did that four times, I at least had money for laundry. Who's the idiot now? Before a meet, Coach gathered the team for a prayer, as I started to join in, he said, "This one isn't for Jewish swimmers." That one really stung because it was in front of the team.

Coach, who was a "born again Christian," called me into his office one day and said, "Hey Gershe, how come Jews don't believe in Jesus?" Uh, hey coach, Jesus was a Jew, I think I win this one. I had to defend Judaism all on my own. It sucked, but I was not going to let them win the battle. Inside though, I had such rage. Even the university was against me as they served bagel and ham sandwiches! C'mon those two don't go together, everyone knows it bagels with lox; and a schmear.

Internally, I wanted to strike back with violence at those who were saying such things, including my coach. I wasn't a violent person, but sometimes it hurts so bad you want to slap the other person straight. Instead I used humor as my weapon of choice, which seemed to work. We live in a different society today where, unfortunately, those who are being bullied strike back with school shootings. I never thought about it on that level, though.

The only time I can remember where I almost became violent was at a party during my senior year. We were drinking and a so-called-friend was very drunk. He just couldn't stop with the anti-Semitic comments. He was just teasing, but it was just getting out of hand. I grabbed a nearby baseball bat and said, "You say one more thing and I'm bashing your head in." Instead of Dolly yelling "MICHAEL!" like she did all those years before in New York, I felt all the eyes glued to us as the crowd wondered what I would do next. The people who heard it were stunned because it was the first time I ever said something like that. Enough was enough. The guy stared at me in fear and then I smiled and started to laugh, "Gotcha!" I said. Everyone was a bit relieved and the party continued as I left. I couldn't be around them anymore that night, as I just couldn't pretend it was okay anymore.

Prior to a big meet in Buffalo, my great-grandmother, Sophie passed away. Grandma Sophie was an incredible person and her death was not entirely shocking considering she was well into her nineties. My father gave me the option of going to the funeral out on Long Island with the rest of the family or staying in Buffalo to swim. I knew finances were an issue and I was torn. I wanted to be there with family but didn't want to put that financial burden on my father.

I decided to swim and even though my coach tried to give me a "pep talk," I swam horribly. During my 1,000-yard race, which is forty lengths of the pool, I just had memories of spending time with Grandma Sophie flowing through my head. I thought about visiting her on South Beach for so many years while I was growing up. I swam so bad; I knew I should have attended her funeral. We ended up getting snowed in and thus another Ashland swim team party ensued. I had a few beers to numb the emotions running through me.

Just like when we lost my grandmother when I was eight, nothing was ever discussed about Grandma Sophie's death. My father never talked about it. It was just like, one day she is here, the next day she's gone. There was never a "How are you doing?" Granted there was no grief counseling back then and God forbid I cry about her death in front of others. But I did when I was alone. There was just no one I felt I could talk to about it. Not my father and definitely not my coach.

During my first philosophy course, I started to question more things about my mother's death. During practice I would take my anger out in the water. I was angry at God for taking my mother and angry at my father for never talking about her. I just thought, as his son, he should share, never realizing the pain my dad carried. Of course, I had a good amount of anger at Harvey for killing my mother and changing my life so drastically. I was nineteen and questioning my own existence. I wondered why I was still alive. I was an infant, all I did was eat, sleep, and poop. What life did I even have at that time? My mother had a life, why kill her and not me? Eventually I learned I was experiencing survivor's guilt for the first time and it would be something that would plague me for years to come.

In my philosophy course, I was drawn to *The Choice* by Og Mandino. It helped me understand my mother's death, a little bit. I won't ruin the book for you, as I highly recommend it, but it was about a father who had to make a "choice" to save his son's life by sacrificing his own. After reading the father's journey, I thought, well, perhaps my mother had a similar journey. When the drunk driver's car was about to hit us, she sacrificed her life to save me. And with Coach Pete years earlier, I learned that with every choice we make, there are consequences. This book gave me some comfort in believing my mother, like any parent would, saved me in that instant. It didn't answer all my questions and certainly didn't give me total peace, but I gained a different perspective which I really needed.

The friendship between Bryan, Brent, Sean, Dennis, Big John and I continued to strengthen during the academic year. We became "the Six-Pack." It felt like our own little private club. We had tons of inside jokes and everyone got abused, either verbally or physically at some point. Giving each other "the finger" for us, was also a symbol of endearment. We loved watching wrestling and would emulate the moves either in our tiny room or out in the hallway. Someone was usually diving off the top bunk into a pile. Often, we left Dennis laying in the hallway after being on the bottom of a routine pile-on.

During Easter weekend of 1990, we traveled to Brent's hometown of Delphos where we proceeded to eat his mom out of house and home. Over the years, the amount of food we ate has grown like a fish story, but we did eat our way through fifty to sixty tacos and about ninety pancakes. As we learned from his recruiting trip, Dennis had a penchant for leaving and going on walks. At one point, it was Dennis' turn to be picked on and he stormed out of the house. As the door slammed behind him, we all just laughed, believing he would be back in a few minutes and yelled, "Don't forget our cheeseburgers this time!" He was in a new, strange town, where would he go anyway? We waited for him for a while, but he never returned.

As we headed out for the night at some club, we ran into another teammate, Eric, who lived close to Delphos. We told him about Dennis walking off. "Guys! I picked him up on the way here! He is across the street," Eric said. Sure enough, there he was. If Dennis wasn't wearing his Ashland Swimming jacket, Eric might not have noticed him.

While we were all in the underage club, Dennis, told us later on, with his famous grin, "I was being served a beer across the street! I was going to hop a train." I truly believe that weekend really cemented our friendship for life. Almost thirty years later, we are still waiting on those cheeseburgers.

Sadly, our little gang would soon breakup. Due to financial reasons, Sean and Dennis were not coming back to Ashland, which was a huge disappointment, considering the bond we formed. Bryan, and I were going to room together in my room. Brent and Big John along with a senior, Randy, aka "Shrubber", were going to live in a triple on the same side of the floor. Shrubber, who got the nickname for working at a plant nursery during the summers, lived next door to Sean and me. I had known Shrubber from my freshman year, but we all became better friends during my sophomore year as neighbors. It turned out that Shrubber and I had the same birthday, but he is three years older.

We finished out my sophomore year in grand style during Springfest, which was the campus' huge party. It had really exciting events and a band. Big John and I represented our dorm at Residence Hall Council. We had to share what our dorm would be doing for the big event. We sat there, with great anticipation, as we listened to what each hall decided to do. When it was our turn, we beamed with pride and said in unison, "We will be doing Jell-O wrestling!" I never saw so many mouths drop open with looks of disgust before in my entire life. We bought a kiddie pool and got Convo to make us two fifty-gallon garbage cans of red Jell-O. We broke the pool pretty quick, but we definitely had a large crowd watching us make fools out of ourselves. It was an amazing time. I was picking Jell-O out of my ears for what seemed like weeks. It was a great way to end the year.

Sean, Me, Brent, Bryan, Big John, Dennis

Top from left: Me, Sean, Dennis

Bottom from left: Brent, Big John, Bryan

Chapter 14

Fish Out of Water

Back home during the summers, I swam for the Hurricanes, the team I wanted to swim for when we left Sheeler-Winton. I also worked as a camp counselor at Magicamp. It was founded by the son of my first agent, who was a well-known local magician. We taught magic and did other day camp activities like bowling and swimming at the University of Miami.

At some point during the summer, my left knee swelled up during swim practice. It was literally three sizes bigger than my right one and would not return to its normal size. I was doing one-legged flip turns due to the pain of pushing off the wall. Turns out, due to all the years of breaststroke, I developed chondromalacia, which is when the cartilage on the underside of the kneecap deteriorates. After resting for a while, the swelling did not go down, so I ended up having arthroscopic surgery to clean it up a couple of weeks before returning to college.

Bryan picked me up at the airport and I was still on crutches which, if you ever used them, know they are not fun. Usually your friends take one or both of them from you and laugh. I felt useless around campus with people helping me with my stuff as I got settled and my knee healed. I would go to the trainers' room and do my physical therapy with little to no supervision. I always felt that swimmers always got ignored in that room.

Coach had his doubts about me swimming again and like usual, when someone says I can't do something, I try my hardest to prove them wrong. When I finally got back into the water, it was a great feeling. The knee was getting stronger with physical therapy and I was happy doing breaststroke again. I could go back to my "me time" in the water. Granted, I was sharing a lane with others, but I was in my own little world. Swimming was my identity.

I was twenty and still trying to find my own path, but at least I was happy. Sean and Dennis were not coming back to school, but we all stayed in touch. Dennis was going to college in New Jersey and Sean was back home in Columbus working. They would come up to visit, which was always fun. Dennis created an imaginary roommate called, "Ty" and I would often call well after midnight waking Dennis up asking if "Ty" was there. It's amazing how we all stayed in touch without the power of social media.

Swimming is supposed to be such a healthy sport, but years of training puts stress on the body. As I found out with my knee. When I got tendonitis in high school in my shoulder, or even the knee situation, we always wondered if it had anything to do with the car crash. No one could really answer that question. We just chalked it up to all the years in the pool. Unfortunately, my reunion with the water was short lived.

A week before the first meet, my right shoulder gave out on me. I was in extreme pain. I could not even raise my arm. The pain wouldn't stop. You know the type of pain that makes you grind your teeth so hard you hope the pain in your jaw makes it goes away? It was that type of agony. I started to rest my shoulder to see if that would help with the pain, but it was too much. At least it gave me an excuse not to raise my hand in class! About three hours prior to our first home meet, I met with Coach in his office to inform him I could not swim.

I was a distance swimmer, swimming the most of anyone with the 1,000-yard freestyle, 200-yard butterfly or breastroke and 500-yard freestyle in most of the meets. No wonder my body was breaking down. We gathered in Convo for a team meeting and I felt horrible for letting my team down. But there was no physical way I could swim with my shoulder like it was. Coach proceeded to embarrass me in front of the team by saying how I couldn't go and who knows if we would even win now. Gee, thanks, Coach. As if I didn't feel bad enough.

I fell into a slight depression and withdrew from the team. As Bryan would get up early for practice, I slept. Sometimes I would sleep on my favorite green couch, that I won in some "clash costume contest" the year before. I had won a gift card to Goodwill and bought a couch that was in the triple with Big John, Brent and Shrubber. It was the best napping couch I ever owned. I also started to indulge a little bit more with alcohol. Not on a daily basis, but it would help with the depression I was feeling. Thanks to a severe deviated septum that pretty much blocked the left side of my nose, I was a mouth breather. I could not chug beers like my friends which in a way I was jealous, but also, relieved.

My grades suffered a bit as I tried to work through the shoulder pain and life away from the pool. I just stayed away because Coach didn't make things any easier for me either. Coaches really want able-bodies in the water and I wasn't one of them. I skipped the annual Christmas training trip and stayed home in Miami to rest. I saw a doctor who prescribed physical therapy.

I told Coach that I was feeling a bit better after some treatment at home and wanted to give it a go. He really didn't want me to swim, but I had to get back into the water. I was limited in the water, and out of shape from what I should have been but felt like myself again.

At this point, I started to get more involved with campus activities. I was already a member of the college radio station, campus activities board and President of Kilhefner Hall. I had Big John as my vice-president which made meetings at Residence Hall Council a lot of fun. Everyone was too serious, and John and I brought, let's just say, life, to the meetings. I may not have been a leader on the swim team, but I was starting to be one on campus where I felt I could make a difference.

At one Residence Hall Council meeting we were told that there was no extra money to fix up the dorms. Kilhefner was probably the worst dorm on campus. Especially the lobby. As my house council was busy painting our TV room, Clark Hall, the woman's dorm across from us, was getting a lovely renovation courtesy of the university. My father once told me a story about him working as a waiter in the Catskills during the summer. He organized a strike because he felt they were not getting paid enough. Granted they all got fired, but he stood up for what he thought was right, and it taught me that one should at least stand up for what you believe in. Even though the outcome may not be what you want. At least go down swinging!

I proceeded to draft a letter to the editor of the newspaper about this travesty. We felt our dorm was being ignored once again for things we thought were essential. Like deadbolts for our doors. You could use your ID card to pretty much get into any room in the building. I even made a video of how to do it in my television class! Why even have a key? How much was too much money to secure our safety?

Big John was not as irate as I was, but he proofread the letter and made sure it was "less angry." The day after it ran in the newspaper, I got a call from the Vice President of Business Affairs requesting a meeting with me. I thought, "Oh great, I'm going to get kicked out of school." I was freaking out a little bit since I had no idea what the meeting was going to be about. When I got to his office, he said, "I read your letter. How can I help make things better?"

I told him, "Our lobby is in shambles and while we don't deny Clark Hall should be fixed up, it seems ours is being overlooked. Have you been in our building lately?" We walked over and discussed all the problems. He was receptive to everything. This taught me a valuable lesson. If we don't stand up for what we believe in, nothing will ever happen. Now, he could have said, "I saw your letter and we won't do anything," but at least we stood up for ourselves. After I graduated, they renovated the lobby and put deadbolts on every door. I can't get in the lobby to see it, but knowing I had something to do with it makes me feel proud.

When it was time for our conference meet in Cleveland, my first race in a month was the five-hundred-yard freestyle. Although my mind was ready, my shoulder rejected the notion pretty quickly. I basically swam with one arm since the right one was useless after one hundred yards. I gained about thirty seconds from my regular time and struggled to get out of the pool. As I floated in the warm down pool, Coach came over to see how I was doing. He said, "Why didn't you just get out of the race if it hurt so bad?" I told him," No way I could quit in the middle of the race, I had to at least finish."

Wrapping my shoulder in ice never felt so good. I swam one more race, the one-hundred-yard breastroke, which was my favorite event. I just wanted to swim one more time, bad shoulder and all. Somehow, I did my personal best time and was thrilled that I didn't quit six months ago. The pain was well worth it for that personal best. I should have bet my Dad and Dolly a Star Wars toy! My junior year in college really put me through a huge test, physically and mentally. As I headed back to Miami for summer break, I was looking forward to my senior year.

Chapter 15

The Final Countdown

For our senior year, Bryan was going to move off campus with another swimmer. Luckily for me, I was the Student Activities Intern. That meant I had my own free room, which was great because I really didn't want a roommate any longer. I had also thought about running for student body president since the other candidate was running unopposed. I thought with swimming, being a Peer Educator, my radio shift, library job, internship, oh, and classes, I was going to be pretty busy. I decided not to run but I found out if I had, I would have won!

While I was home for the summer, I got an MRI on my right shoulder. The results showed a torn rotator cuff along with some damaged tendons. No wonder I was in so much pain all the time. After resting from swimming during the summer, I decided to have surgery. Like the year before, it was done a couple of weeks prior to returning to college. A doctor who worked with athletes from the University of Miami would oversee the operation. Unlike with my knee, the shoulder surgery was not necessarily for swimming, but to make sure I fixed the rotator cuff to have a normal life. Last year I returned to campus on crutches, this year it was with my arm in a sling.

The semester began and I found myself going to class, working in the library and diving into my internship. It seemed like Deja vu as I headed to the basement of the gym for physical therapy. Bryan and I were the only two senior men on the team, and I felt distant from the team, because I wasn't swimming yet. I did my physical therapy until I was ready to hop back into the pool. Coach once again did not believe I was ready to swim, and I hate to say it, he was right. I was impatient, and I probably should have taken a bit longer to do physical therapy. Despite this, I just had to test the shoulder in the pool. I missed being a swimmer. I needed to feel myself in the water again. I missed the competition and my sense of identity.

The shoulder was a little sore, but I didn't feel the pain as I did earlier in the year. The team was pretty supportive of me during our first meet in October 1991. It was an invitational at Bowling Green State University. I wasn't in the best of shape, but I felt good enough to swim. After my first race, the two-hundred-yard freestyle, reality finally began to set in. I was in too much pain and rushed to get back into the water. Practice is one thing, but when you have the adrenaline flowing through your veins in the heat of competition, it is another. It was my first race since in months and I had to prove something to myself. My biggest fear was that I just undid everything the surgery was meant to do: give me a better life after swimming.

On the bus ride home, I realized that life without swimming was going to be my fate. I was taking pain medication as if they were Flintstone Vitamins. I did not let on to anyone how much pain I was in. I continued to take pain killers, sometimes with alcohol—not my finest decision making, I know.

I would stare out the little narrow window of my room on the second floor and wanted to jump. Swimming was my identity and now I wasn't going to be a swimmer anymore. I realized I had to quit something for the first time, and I felt I was losing myself. Who would I be now? I had been a swimmer since age four and now it was all over. Talk to any athlete and they will tell you, quitting is the hardest thing to do, especially due to an injury. I wanted to go out on my terms not because my body failed me.

Instead, I watched the team through the viewfinder of the video camera for a while as I filmed our meets. I was so depressed that I could not swim, and eventually stopped filming.

I thought the pain from my shoulder was bad but being on that deck not swimming was even worse. I'm not even sure I told Coach that I was going to stop showing up. I just walked away. It was so traumatic; I even wrote about the death of my swimming career in my "Death and Dying" course for my final paper.

Swimming gave me so many opportunities in life, including an education That chapter was about to close but a new one was about to be written. Being hurt gave me an opportunity to go down a different path that eventually led to *The Magic of Life*. Of course, I didn't know it at that time.

Instead of the pool, my role as Peer Educator was shaping my future in ways I did not expect. I knew if I was going to be someone who promoted a healthier lifestyle, then I had to walk the talk. Did I drink in college? Yes, but it wasn't like I partied every single day. Now that I was twenty-one—I already did my fair share the previous three years—it just didn't have the same attraction anymore. Earlier in the semester I used alcohol to drink away my sorrows about swimming, but that was about it. I would still go to the local bar and have a couple drinks, but nothing like my first three years. My friends had limited knowledge about the drunk driving crash. With my experience in student activities, I thought about doing a program about it. How could I share my story with people? Being a Peer Educator gave me that opportunity.

The first time I spoke publicly about the car crash was in Kilhefner's second floor lobby during my senior year. And when I say publicly, it was in front of my friends, Big John, Bryan, and Kevin, who had lost his brother due to a drunk driver. There were a couple of other people as well. I was in front of my friends, but it was very, very scary. "My father was driving us home," I said. "I was just an infant…"

I could feel my vocal cords tighten when I talked about the car crash. My voice remained steady as I walked them through the crash and its aftermath. In moments like this, you can hear the emotion in your voice as you witness the look in people's eyes reflect their reaction.

"I knew about your mom, but never knew how much it affected you," Big John said, his eyes soft.

"We unfortunately share the experience of losing a family member," my friend Kevin said. "I know how you feel."

It's one thing to say, "My mom is dead due to a car crash," to one person, but to express how it felt to a group of people was a vulnerable experience. The presentation was less about the dangers of alcohol and more about drunk driving. I believe the message really hit home. If we did go to the Flats in Cleveland, I would drive because I would be the sober one, which was perfectly fine with me. It was my responsibility to make sure we got home safely.

As I was wrapping up my senior year, I still had no idea what I really was going to do after I graduated. I still had my mind set on being a magician and pursuing comedy. I was still going to use my Communications degree for that. I saw performers and speakers on the college circuit and thought I could do it as well. I enjoyed being a student leader on campus and knew how much my advisers changed my life. Perhaps working on a college campus was my future.

During spring break, I applied for a Residence Hall Director job at the University of Miami. When they asked if I had a Master's degree, my thought was, "Oh, I'm supposed to have one of those? Great, now more school!" With my student organization experience, I thought about going into Higher Education but did not know much about it other than from my residence director, Dermot, who was getting his Master's degree from Bowling Green in Higher Education Administration. Graduation was coming up soon, but when Easter weekend came, all that was in jeopardy.

I was staying with Big John at his home in Lakewood, a suburb on the west side of Cleveland. He wanted a bouncer job in the Flats during the summer, so we started to walk to each bar as he filled out applications. I began to feel ill and no, it had nothing to do with walking around Cleveland, it's a nice city. At first, we just thought it was the flu and Big John was kind enough to give me his room down in the basement instead of the couch. His mom, Beverly, also known as "The Bev," was awesome and made me soup and Jell-O. Upon returning to campus, my fever didn't go down and my throat was also causing a lot of pain. My Dad would call frequently to see how I was doing and when my condition failed to change after a day or two, he started to get worried. I was in the showers trying to get my temperature down when I heard someone calling my name. It was a campus security guard that found me after my father called them.

I was taken to the hospital where I was diagnosed with mono and strep throat. I was never so happy to get a shot in the butt before! The weekend coming up was Springfest which was always our last "party" before finals. I was recovering in my room as Big John snuck a keg into his room. He kept checking up on me, or as he put it, "I want to make sure you're still alive." I missed nearly two weeks of classes and even got food delivered to me from the Director of the Health Center, which I thought was really nice. My professors worked with me and I just had to take my finals in order to graduate. I was already a skinny person, weighing one hundred and fifty pounds, but with mono and strep throat, I lost about twenty of those pounds. My cap and gown looked really big on me!

My Dad, Dolly and Jeff came for graduation which was held outside on campus. It was a bittersweet feeling to be done with four years of hard work (okay, semi-hard work in classes.) Despite dealing with anti-Semitism and the injuries that caused my early retirement from swimming, I was happy with the person I'd become in those four short years. From the pain I experienced from being called "Jesus Killer" to the first time processing my mother's death and my own survival, these things had a great impact on my life.

Somewhere along the four years, I discovered I never wanted to go through what my father went through in losing my mother. I had built a wall around me to protect me from a hurt like that. I hid my depression when I stopped swimming and I also hid my thoughts about my mother's death deep within me. All that pain was stuffed into a corner, like my father had done. People knew me as the "happy go lucky" guy who could make them laugh, and that is the image I portrayed. But that was just the outside. Inside, no one knew I was a tortured soul.

I also found a purpose and a new identity during my senior year. Even though I had shared my story in that lobby to a few friends, it became something I wanted to pursue. I discovered a lot about myself, from questioning God about my mother's death to my own mortality. The brotherhood with Bryan, Sean, Dennis, Brent, Big John and I was an added bonus of college that provided a ton of priceless memories. As I was preparing to leave campus for good, I realized how much I changed during the last four years. While I was still unsure of my future, Ashland University gave me an education not just in the classroom, but also within myself.

Graduating from Ashland University, May 1992

Chapter 16
I Graduated, Now What?

After graduation, I returned to my childhood home in Miami. Still recovering from mono, there was no rush to find a job. I was told to rest, but I wanted to continue performing magic and really kick off my comedy career. Realistically, working on a college campus would be a solid career choice though. Before I joined the "real world" I wanted to have a fun job doing something I had never done before. I saw an advertisement for a camp counselor at a Jewish camp in the Poconos.

When I interviewed for the job, we discussed my background as a magician, and they asked if I was interested in teaching magic to the campers. I was so excited about the opportunity since I had taught magic during previous summers. I was going to be in a cabin with ten- and eleven-year-old boys and for the first time ever, be in the "wilderness." I worked with the camp owner to order some tricks and taught magic lessons for those who wanted to learn.

Jeff was living in South Jersey at this time, so after a quick visit, I took the bus from his place to the camp in

East Stroudsburg, Pennsylvania. I just spent four years in Ashland, a small town like East Stroudsburg, and that learning experience gave me a different perspective on people, especially in smaller towns.

Before camp started, two other counselors from Miami and I decided to head to the local mall. They decided to look "Miami tough" in this little town mall wearing identical tight pink bike shorts and white t-shirts. They thought they looked cool, but I thought they looked like fools. I stayed ten paces behind them in my KISS shirt, comfortable in my own skin. I still remember the people in the mall staring at them with facial expressions that clearly said, "What the hell are those two wearing and why?"

At the start of camp, there was a "hide and go seek" game where counselors hid on the camp's grounds. Unbeknownst to me, counselors were assigned a point value, which was chosen based on popularity. Which if you think about it, is absurd at the start of camp, because no one really knows anyone. The counselors who returned from previous years were assigned a higher point value by staff members who knew them.

After I was caught, I discovered I was only worth 200 points, one of the lowest levels. Talk about a shot to the ego! At the mid-way point of camp when new campers came in, we played again. I was found, in what I thought was a perfect hiding spot by the horses. Unlike the beginning of camp, I had the highest score of the counselors. I guess being myself and working with the campers paid off. I totally immersed myself in camp life, well, maybe not the matzo pizza though, but all the other aspects.

As we prepared for "Color Wars," a game between the campers, some of the counselors went into town for cheap beer night. I stayed and worked with the campers. I already did my cheap beer drinking in college, I wasn't interested in doing it again. Besides, I was there for the campers and had way more fun with the few counselors that did stay behind with me. I enjoyed my time teaching magic, sitting by the lake and getting to know some of the other counselors from abroad.

I repelled into a cave, experienced a laundromat eating my money, and got acquainted with nature. Yours truly also participated in a counselor "drag" contest where

I strutted around to KISS' *I Was Made for Loving You.* Some of the female campers really enjoyed doing my makeup. Oddly enough, pictures of that day disappeared for this book. Funny how that happens. I was glad I made the decision to be a camp counselor in the summer and gained new experiences in life.

When camp was over in August 1992, I stayed with Dennis in New Jersey and was scheduled to fly home on August 24th. The only problem was that Hurricane Andrew visited Miami that day. Coincidentally, Sean was visiting Dennis as well, so it was great to see my old roommate. We went into New York to catch a double header at Yankee Stadium along with Dennis' childhood friend, Tom. Throughout the day we joked that I may not have a home to go to as I couldn't reach my parents. In all honesty, I was completely frightened of that reality.

Two days later I flew into Miami International Airport. As I looked out the window, I was in awe as I took in the destruction from the plane. You know how people say it looks like a bomb went off after a massive hurricane? That is exactly how Miami looked.

On the drive home, landmarks were gone, homes disappeared, and there was no power. You just couldn't prepare yourself for the magnitude of the damage from Andrew. Luckily, my cousin Steven was able to drive down from Okeechobee with a generator and supplies, including a "Miami Vice style" cell phone that looked like a brick.

I didn't know what to expect when we made it to my street. The stop sign at the corner was dangling upside down from the pole. Someone found the street marker and hammered it about a foot off the ground. My Dad and Dolly did not evacuate during the storm. They huddled together in a closet. The brown front doors blew inward and went flying through the living room and out the back-sliding glass doors. The front windows of my room were also blown out and parts of the roof were missing. Miraculously a KISS poster that was the size of a door remained on the wall with just a small tear. The carpet was already pulled up and discarded due to the water damage. Both Jeff's and my bed were destroyed, but luckily, we had an extra bed in another bedroom I could use. The screen that was over the pool was probably in another county. We wondered where the basketball pole that was on our driveway went. It was unbelievable.

Without power or a land-line phone it was extremely difficult to make any headway. I continued to help my father clean up the area. I got to use a chainsaw for the first time on some trees, which was pretty fun. After I used it my father asked me if I had all my fingers.

The heat and humidity were unbearable without air conditioning, but at least we had the generator to power up fans and some lights. I would wake up when the generator ran out of gas, causing the house to get eerily quiet. Food for squirrels was scarce since the trees were bare from the wind damage, so I would buy peanuts and hand feed them. They would take one, scurry off to bury it and come back for another one.

The organ my dad loved to play was damaged beyond repair and that was pretty disheartening.

Due to people looting places and homes, my dad got a gun for protection. I joked with him, "Dad we have nothing left, what will they steal?" Fortunately, he never had to use it. Going to the range with him was a good bonding moment, though. My dad was a pretty good shot.

We finally got our phone and power restored about three weeks after the storm. I called all the guys to let them know how things were going. While they were progressing with their lives, mine was on hold due to Hurricane Andrew.

Two months after Andrew, in October, it was time to finally look for a job. While it wasn't exactly higher education, I became the Activities Director for the EF International School of English. The school was located at the north campus of Florida International University.

Some of the students lived on campus for a nine-month experience and some people stayed at apartments for a shorter tenure to learn English. While it was thirty miles from me, the campus was only a couple of miles from my grandfather's place, so I would occasionally stay at his condo instead of making the long drive back to the house. Driving in Miami is an adventure and sometimes the drive would take anywhere from one to two hours.

It was the perfect job for a recent college graduate because I would incorporate things I did in college with the international students. My main responsibility was to organize activities on campus and to book local travel trips for the students. We had BBQs, pumpkin carving events, and I introduced them to American culture, while in turn, I learned their cultures too. Some of the trips booked were to Nassau, Jamaica, Mexico, and Disney World, which was a lot of fun. I had a wonderful time being their "chaperone" on these trips.

I also got Sean an interview for a Resident Assistant position that he eventually turned down to stay in Columbus. With Big John the only one left at Ashland, I would send him postcards of my travels with messages unsuitable to print in this book. Big John was in Ohio, learning, and I was on some beach somewhere enjoying my job. It was the least I could do. Oh yes, it was horrible I tell you, horrible. It was fun, but I still found myself missing my friends in Ohio.

I was using Dolly's car for a while for work, but we all soon realized it was time for me to grow up and get my first car. My Dad helped me shop and did most of the talking. I ended up buying a silver Mercury Tracer. The only features I really cared about was that it had a cassette player and that it was not damaged by Hurricane Andrew.

Throughout my life I have always wondered if my mother looked over me. And in late 1992, I got my answer. I was on my way to work one morning, heading north on the busy Miami freeway, 826, in the Hialeah area. If you have ever driven on it between the hours of 7 a.m. and 10 a.m., you know that you use up your quota of swear words for the day. The car in front of me swerved to avoid a car that was in the left emergency lane which was also protruding out into the left lane. I swerved as well, but over compensated and lost control of my car. To be honest, I was probably going 5 mph over the speed limit and soon found myself facing southbound traffic on the northbound side. It happened quickly yet it felt like I was going in slow motion in my brain. I took my foot off the gas and did a one-hundred-eighty-degree spin, hitting the guardrail with my rear bumper.

I am not sure how cars did not slam into me since it was the morning rush hour. When I finally got to work, my co-workers said I was as white as a ghost. My Miami tan faded after the crash. How I didn't die on that freeway is something I cannot explain. Just like how my mother protected me from that drunk driving crash years ago, she must have done it once again. Somehow, I escaped with just a bruised ego and a damaged bumper.

In December of 1992, we ended up getting a trailer to live in while our house was being renovated. Shopping for a trailer was fun while we played with all the features. But we quickly discovered just how close those quarters were with three people living in there! When squirrels jumped on the roof, we would hear a loud *thud.* When my father sneezed, the trailer would shake! I was on one side with bunk beds and the birds on the floor while my Dad and Dolly inhabited the other side. It definitely was tight quarters, but we did what we had to in order to survive.

I was still enjoying my time working with the international students when I found out that The University of Akron had a graduate program for higher education. I was thrilled that I found a school relatively close to Ashland, but really nervous about taking the GRE entrance exam. I was never any good at those standardized tests and was stressed because I knew I could do well in a master's program, despite the test. I submitted my resume for an assistantship that would help pay for school and offer me more experience in the field. Due to my GPA and

GRE score, I was provisionally accepted, which meant I had to earn a 3.0 each semester to keep my assistantship. I knew if I stayed focused, I could do that easily.

I interviewed for the student activities assistantship right after playing sand volleyball one day. During the interview, as I dusted sand off of me, I thought, "Do I really want to go back to Ohio?" Unfortunately, I did not get that assistantship, but they created a student leadership adviser assistantship with me in mind due to my background in student government and leadership roles at Ashland. Now I had to make the hard decision - return to Ohio or continue living in a trailer with my parents. Returning to Ohio just made sense for my future and I accepted the assistantship.

After graduating from Ashland, I still wanted to pursue being a college entertainer with a focus on alcohol abuse and drunk driving. I believed that working in higher education would get me closer to my goal. With our international students, alcohol was a part of their culture, but we did not want them getting hurt or driving drunk while in Miami. I approached the director of the school and asked if I could do a program for the students about alcohol, but more specifically, drunk driving.

I revamped some of the magic tricks like the "needle thru the balloon" and turned it into how alcohol affects your body. The needle would symbolize alcohol and if you drank it too quickly, your stomach could explode. I thought I was on cutting edge material, not Shakespeare mind you, but I thought it was better than the "patter" you get with the tricks when you buy it in the store. Writing new material for the tricks that pertained to the dangers of alcohol reminded me of being in SADD back in high school.

My Dad and Dolly attended the program which made me a little nervous since I would be talking about the crash with students. Even though the students were learning English, they definitely understood how drunk driving could impact their lives after knowing how it changed my life. Prior to the presentation, they only knew me as their activities director, but soon after they knew me as someone different. Hearing my story really affected the students, which was my goal. In the spring of 1993, although it didn't have a title yet, *The Magic of Life*, was born.

In July 1993, after a trip to Jamaica with students, I packed up my car including my magic and left the home I grew up in for good. I left the birds behind, since I didn't know exactly where I was going to live and hoped they would be okay without me. I had saved up a little bit for graduate school but would survive mostly on student loans and my stipend. I was pretty fortunate to have the assistantship pay for my tuition for the next two years.

I was anxious and yet nervous as I would embark on this new adventure. I made a stop in Nashville to see Bryan on my drive up north which was great. My final destination would be Big John's house which was actually behind the Burger King in Ashland. Yes, the one that didn't exist yet during my college recruitment trip. The house was nicknamed "The BK House." Big John let me stay with him until I found a place in Akron. I was looking forward to returning to Ohio and while I wasn't thrilled about homework again, I was excited about the assistantship.

Chapter 17
Hello Akron

Upon reaching the now familiar town of Ashland, I was relegated to sleeping on a couch at the "BK House" for a few days. I made the 45-minute drive to Akron and formally introduced myself to my new supervisor, Sandra. Since I was clueless about where to live, she recommended Channelwood Village, a fixed income building not too far away from campus. I found a small one-bedroom apartment on the fifteenth floor for $289 per month including utilities. It was perfect! I just needed a bed, furniture, kitchenware and everything else essential to live as a functioning adult. My college neighbor Shrubber lived fairly close by and helped since he had a truck. It was good to be near my friends again as I prepared for two more years of school.

Maintaining that 3.0 would be easy. I may have been close to my friends again, but I did not know anyone else in Akron. That meant less distractions so I could focus on my studies. There were three other graduate assistants in the office. I would work twenty hours a week, advising student government along with

Sandra, and organize events for student leaders, plus go to class. I was learning about the history of college and trying to answer questions such as, "Are leaders born or are they made?" What do you think?

The Six-Pack had its first milestone with a wedding in the fall of 1993. Brent would tie the knot and we were all his groomsmen. The night before the big day, being the mature individuals, that we were, we held a massive pillow fight and wrestling match in the hotel. I am pretty sure Sean gave Big John a concussion. Also, we might have, or might not have broken a bed from our shenanigans. Brent was heading off to Basic Training for the Army right after the wedding and unfortunately the marriage did not last long. We were all in our early 20s and still had a lot to of growing up to do.

Over Christmas break I flew home to Miami. The house repairs were still unfinished. My Dad ended up getting screwed over by some contractors, so things were slow to get fixed. The poor birds on the floor in "my room" of the trailer were neglected as Mickey's beak had grown a few more inches. The tip of his beak curved and almost touched his chest! I was pretty upset because neither my Dad nor Dolly noticed it. I couldn't understand how they didn't see him like that. I don't even know how he ate or moved in his cage with that beak. Apparently, they just changed the water and food, without even looking at him. Luckily a vet was able to trim his beak back to normal length and gave him a physical, whatever the hell that is for a bird. I mean, if you coughed, Mickey would cough too, but I have a feeling it wasn't the same thing. I decided to take the birds back with me on the plane. I couldn't leave them behind this time.

My first academic year in graduate school went pretty well and I really enjoyed my job with the students. During the summer of 1994, since I was only taking one class plus working with the Orientation department, I got a job as a swim coach for a local team. Coaching along with performing magic at birthday parties would bring in some much-needed money. I would walk the side of the pool like Coach Peter, embracing his spirit which rubbed some swimmers the wrong way. I never threw a kickboard at them, though. They were swimming for enjoyment rather than competition. I was told by the head coach to turn down my "enthusiasm."

My "enthusiasm" for life was waning. Things were going fairly well, but for some reason, I started to think about my mother. I remembered what someone told me when my grandmother died; that one day I would see her again. But this time, I wanted to meet my mother. These feelings led me into a slight depression. I thought about survivor's guilt and my own existence again. I portrayed an "everything is fine" appearance, but mentally something was wrong. The pain washed over me. It was overwhelming and much stronger than what I felt when I had to stop swimming. I had no pain killers to take for this pain. It had nothing to do with my body and everything to do with my soul.

It was a warm breezy summer evening when I stepped onto the balcony and looked down at the cars below. I wondered what it would feel like to fly through the air. Would it ease this pain I was feeling? Why was it so strong?

I didn't even know why the pain was there, it just was. And it wasn't like life was horrible for me at this time. I was enjoying graduate school. I was close to my friends. Yet for the life of me, I was terribly depressed, and I couldn't figure out why.

I was twenty-three and wanted to meet my mother. Jumping off that balcony seemed like a pretty good way to do it. I dove off the blocks for swimming, I could just dive off the balcony and ruin someone's car down below. I just wanted to stop feeling the pain.

I went to bed convinced I would jump in the morning. I gave myself at least one more good sleep. I wasn't even sure what I would write in a note or if I would even write one.

That night, I had a dream where my mother came to me. I heard a voice and saw my mother's image. It felt as real as you are holding this book in your hands right now. Her voice was soft and calm. She said, "Michael, stop worrying about me, I'm fine." Then she gave me a hug which felt so warm and comforting. I suddenly woke up, face down in the pillow with my arms crossed as if I was hugging my mother. Needless to say, I didn't jump, and that dream was a great reminder for me. Whenever I did get to a low point, I couldn't do something stupid.

A few days later on July 4th, 1994, I was hanging out with Sean and Big John in Ashland. On the drive down, I debated telling them about how I was feeling about the unforgettable dream I had. I figured if anyone would understand the loss of a parent, it would be those two since they also had parents die when they were young. Sean and John both lost their fathers, but we never really talked about how it affected us.

We were outside standing by the fence having a beer, discussing life. We weren't exactly kids anymore and the thought of telling them was scary. Men don't talk about depression, right?

With Big John and Sean's back against the fence, I looked at them and said, "We have a special bond since we all lost a parent and never knew them. Last night I was thinking about my mother and felt like I wanted to meet her. I'm feeling down, and I don't know why. I thought about jumping off my balcony and destroying someone's car down below." I could feel the lump in my throat grow with each word because we were used to insulting each other. We didn't talk about this type of stuff. Big John's reaction was so emotional and raw.

Upon hearing my confession, he turned to face the fence and kicked the bottom of five panels right off the fence and onto the ground. He did it with such ease, it was enough for me to see what I meant to him and Sean. We did a group hug like men and I realized, I couldn't do that to them. My mother didn't sacrifice her life so I could take mine. I couldn't do it to my family. The thought of my Dad burying me was not something I could bear.

When the fall semester started in 1994, I was ready for the academic year. Not only was I advising student government but added BACCHUS (Boosting Alcohol Consciousness Concerning the Health of University Students) adviser to my title as well. I was a member of the organization as a Peer Educator at Ashland and they needed an adviser at Akron. During this semester, one of my students in student government, who knew my background with drunk driving asked, "Can you put on a fun alcohol program for my sorority?" Why yes, yes, I can!

I came up with the title, *The Magic of Life* since I was using magic tricks to convey the messages about the dangers of alcohol. While it was similar to the one I did for the international students, my new knowledge of Higher Education and experience as the BACCHUS adviser, helped me gear the program to address issues facing college students. It was a great blend of magic, my story, and facts on how alcohol impacts each student. The students really enjoyed it. While talking about the car crash still terrified me, knowing it made a difference made my sweaty palms and stomach-churning worth it.

In 1994, the second Six-Pack wedding occurred. Bryan married his college girlfriend, Tina, who was also a swimmer at Ashland. I ended up being his best man which was a great honor. I was so nervous that I would lose the rings and kept on making sure they were in my pocket during the ceremony. I didn't want to be *that* guy and lose them on their big day. Brent flew in from Texas where he was stationed, but Dennis could not make it in from New Jersey due to a work commitment. Sean and Big John were also Bryan's groomsmen for the big day in Mansfield, Ohio. Their wedding was a nice stress reliever from the fall semester.

It was my final semester of graduate school in January 1995, when a chance encounter would put me back on the comedy stage again. One of my classmates, Lucy, was the booker for Hilarities, the local comedy club. There are days when you second guess if you made the right decisions in life. People often questioned me returning to Ohio, but once again, fate proved itself to be very real once I met Lucy. My childhood dream of being a comedian was in sight. I talked to her after class about being a magician and shared insights from my two previous attempts of performing comedy. I didn't want to perform magic on stage though, just pure stand-up comedy. She told me about open mic night and that I could call the club to set up a date. I was scheduled on February 20, 1995.

Brent's wedding – we look dapper!

Chapter 18

"Hello Mom, it's me, Michael."

For my first comedy open mic, I invited my friends to the show since we had to bring at least ten people to Hilarities to be able to go on stage. Bryan and Tina came up along with students in the organizations I advised. I was a lot more confident in my ability than I was when I was eighteen. I wanted to see how my material would hold up in a comedy club. I was nervous and excited, but I tried to remain calm. In the line-up there was a guy named Tommy from North Canton who was doing it for his second time. We would eventually find out that our fathers went to the same high school together in New York. The showroom manager, Tim, called us all together to give us the open mic speech that laid out the rules for the night.

I wished I remembered my Dad's advice that he had given me for my Bar Mitzvah speech to "*slow down*" because I rushed through my five-minute set. But still got a lot more laughs than I did in my previous attempts back in Miami. I was so thrilled; I felt my comedy dream was finally alive. It was such an amazing high hearing those laughs. It wasn't the *Tonight Show*, but to perform comedy after waiting four years was incredible. Being funny with your friends is one thing but being funny on stage in front of strangers is another. I did such a good job; I got a call back for another open mic when I was done. I was ecstatic!

The only issue with my second appearance at the comedy club was that it was on the night of a group presentation for class. My group was to go last, and I would be missing my stage time. Would my comedy future be derailed by class? Notice my priorities in my last semester of graduate school. Group project or five minutes of stage time? Talk about comedic timing. Fortuitously, I had a really great relationship with my professor, Dr. Dubick and he let our group go first. Right after we were done, I high tailed it to the comedy club for my second set and missed the rest of the group presentations.

In April, a month before I was to graduate with my master's degree, my grandfather, Papa Ben, passed away. My father booked my flight and I swear he never told me which airport I was to depart from. So, when I got to Cleveland Hopkins, there was no flight for me. Turns out I was leaving from Akron instead. I am not sure how I didn't get a speeding ticket, but I barely made my flight. The funny thing is, I once drove to the wrong airport for an interview, months earlier, so my father and Jeff just chalked it up to another "Michael is an idiot" experience. There are a few of those in the books. That one was on me, but this one was on my Dad. But for years after, he and my brother always asked if I knew which airport I was flying out of.

Sadly, Papa Ben, who was diabetic, passed away when I was flying to Miami. My father, Jeff, Dolly and I, drove in silence to the hospital from the airport. While I didn't have a chance to say goodbye to him prior to his passing, I was given a chance to spend a little time with him in the room. I sat with the man who meant so much to me. He was kind, generous, and I never heard him say a bad thing about anyone. He was the one who got Dolly to stay in America when she could have gone back to Jamaica.

He always had a stack of books in his room from the library and I inherited his love for reading. I remember he smoked a pipe then moved on to cigars and, when he stopped smoking them, he would chew on them for the flavor. He taught me how to shoot pool and took me to a lot of movies. But perhaps most of all, he took me to that magic shop which was instrumental in my love for performing comedy and developing *The Magic of Life*. That magic helped this kid in speech therapy gain confidence when speaking in front of people. Without his influence on my life, who knows who I would be.

I was twenty-four years old and about to visit the family plot for the first time, where my mother was laid to rest. The play I wrote six years earlier when I was a freshman in college was about to become reality. I had no idea what to expect, or how I would react. When my grandmother passed away, my father probably thought I was too young to attend her funeral. But as we made our way to Beth Moses Cemetery on Long Island, I was tense, and anxious to finally stand before my mother's headstone.

When we got there, my father found out they opened the wrong plot for my grandfather so the reunion with my mother had a slight delay. When they finally had the right spot ready, we walked quietly to the family plot. My stomach was churning but, oddly enough, I also felt a sense of peace. I thought to myself, *Wow, I'm finally getting a chance to 'meet' my mother.* I saw the great big "GERSHE" family head stone. You know the videos all over the internet of the kids running to greet their parents who are in the military? That is what I wanted to do when I saw my mother's resting place. Instead I remained as calm as I could and walked slowly with everyone else. Despite my display of self-control, I felt like pushing everyone out of the way so I could get there first.

Before the ceremony started for my grandfather, I finally stood before my mother. I looked down at her footstone: "Barbara Gershe - beloved wife, mother and daughter." I whispered to myself, "Hello Mom, it's me, Michael." I could feel my eyes water as I just wanted to sit down and stay there for a long, long time.

We placed rocks , which is a Jewish custom, on her footstone along with my grandmother and great aunt prior to the burial service for my grandfather. During the ceremony, we had a chance to say something as we put fresh dirt on his coffin. I was surprised that I was the only one who wanted to say anything. As I put the shovel into the mound of dirt and gently tossed it onto his coffin I said, "Thank you Papa Ben. Thank you for taking me to that magic store because I wouldn't be the person I am today if you didn't do that."

I was so emotional; I hardly got those words out.

After the ceremony, I stood in front of my mother's stone again, talking with her. I was telling her about my life. I wanted her to feel proud of the person I had become. I turned to my left and noticed my father sitting on a bench a few feet away looking at her footstone. I don't know how long he was even there because I was so caught up in having time with her. I said goodbye to my mother and promised to be back soon. I wanted my father to have his alone time with her. I walked to the car leaving him deep in thought. The image of him staring at my mother's footstone contributed to building that isolating wall around me in my relationships. As we departed the cemetery, the car ride was quiet. Even in the months after Papa Ben's passing, his passing, his death and grieving process was not something discussed.

Instead of taking time to grieve for my grandfather, I had to focus on my classes and think about what I was going to do after graduation. It was quickly approaching. I attended a higher education conference where I interviewed for several jobs in a large conference hall. It was like a feeding frenzy with so many employers and prospective employees. I thought it was a bit stressful because everyone wanted a job and you would sit so close to the next person; you could hear their answers in their interview. You really had to focus. Despite getting to do a few interviews, I still just wanted to pursue comedy and present *The Magic of Life*.

Graduation was approaching in May. I had several more open mic spots and felt myself grow as a comedian. Tim, the showroom manager, always gave me advice. The other comedians I watched when they performed shared words of wisdom as well. Tim always told me to be ready to go on stage. One night as I was standing by the sound room, I heard the intro music signaling the show was about to start. "You're going up to do five minutes," Tim said.

Who had time to panic? I was ready and eager to be on that stage. When I was onstage, nothing else mattered except getting those laughs. Comedy was the drug I needed in my life. It was my great escape from reality.

Prior to graduation, I had to pass my comprehensive exam. I never studied so hard in my life. I knew everything I learned forwards, backwards and upside down. I felt confident, but I also knew the last two years came down to this exam. We were given two questions and had three hours to write in these little "blue books" which made me feel like I was back in elementary school. I passed my comps with A's and I earned my Master's degree in Higher Education Administration. Not bad for a guy that daydreamed through school and was told by several teachers that I never applied myself.

One of my exam questions was on policy. I wrote about the failed alcohol policy implemented at Ashland during my sophomore year. My professor loved it so much she showed it to her husband and gave me the highest score out of my class. See? I could be a great student if I put my mind to it.

My Dad, Dolly and Jeff made their second trip to Ohio to see me graduate. I was happy that Dennis came out from New Jersey. He was joined by Bryan, Tina, Kevin and Sean for the graduation ceremony. Sean also attended Big John's graduation from Ashland earlier in the day. It took Big John six years to graduate and that day was one of his proudest moments. Dennis and I drove down a bit later to celebrate with John and Sean after I finished up celebrating with my family.

After graduation I stayed in Ohio to focus on comedy while actively looking for jobs in higher education. Yes, I know, not the best financial plan after working so hard to earn my master's degree, but comedy was my dream and I was finally doing it.

Most parents would say, "Are you crazy? Forget comedy! You go find a job!" But my father and Dolly supported me knowing that it had been my dream all along.

My first time at Hilarities Comedy Club in Cuyahoga Falls, OH

2/20/1995

I was 24 when I visited my mother for the first time

Jeff's favorite picture with us and Papa Ben

Dad, Papa Ben, Jeff and me

Jeff, Me, Dolly and Dad as I graduated from
The University of Akron with my Master's Degree, May 1995

Hey Dad, I'm going into comedy!

Chapter 19

Chasing Comedy and Flipping Burgers

With my career in higher education postponed, I found a "temp" job working for a local audiologist who specialized in hearing aids. I was more of a receptionist working behind the glass at the front desk. It was pretty easy, and my boss was nice. She taught me quite a bit about hearing aids. I also found a part-time job working for a company that did carnival style games and concession stands. I remember working the lemonade stand for an event and smashing my fingers in the lemonade squeezer several times. I didn't stay much longer with that company.

A few months after my first open mic night I earned my first paid week as an opener. Oddly enough it was with two comedians that I saw when I was an audience member six months prior to this monumental experience.

I was now a paid comedian. Being the host and opening act was scary because not only did I have to perform, but I was responsible for announcements and introducing the other comedians correctly. The two I worked with were both helpful and supportive. I soaked up any advice they would offer just like I did when I was learning magic as a kid. Unlike my Dad's reminder for my Bar Mitzvah to "slow down" I spoke too fast, due to my nerves, on that first night. But by the end of the week, I was a lot more comfortable.

In the fall of 1995, I was hired at a new Fuddruckers for what I thought would be a "leadership/manager" type of job. With my master's degree hanging up on my wall, I was working morning prep work along with cash register, shake maker and expeditor of food. I later worked the grill, fries, cleaned up tables and washed dishes. I figured it would only be temporary until I was working full time as a comedian. I was doing some more shows here and there, trying to make my way in the business.

I relished the times I worked as a dishwasher. When I had enough of customers, I could take any aggression I might have on silverware in the back. People would return food almost completely eaten and say, "This burger is not cooked right." The sarcastic comedian side of me wanted to say something snarky in response.

Working at Fuddruckers made my father's comment from when I was a kid come true—I was flipping burgers for a job.

It was not a great time for me financially. Bills were stacking up and soon I would have to start paying back student loans. Big John got a job at Syracuse University as an assistant equipment manager and would make fun of me because I had two college degrees and was working at Fuddruckers. He was making more money than me and never let me forget it. I felt like a failure in a way, but it was what I chose, and it was up to me to change it. I was not ready to give up comedy just yet and found stage time wherever I could. I was grateful that I lived in a cheap apartment during this time because it was the only place I could afford.

In 1996, I attended a National Association of Campus Activities (NACA) conference as a speaker. I submitted a proposal for one of their lecture showcases and was selected to present the program for students and advisers who book programs. I knew that if you wanted to be a speaker on the college market, this conference was the place to be. I even had my own booth for the exhibit hall where I proudly displayed my four, eleven-by-fourteen sheets of paper marketing *The Magic of Life*. While other companies had elaborate booths, I was on a strict budget and could not afford anything more. By budget, I mean a budget of zero. Zip. Nada.

I was thrilled to be there even though my booth was bare. The company next to me had promotional marketing items and their booth was littered with a plethora of products. There was quite a difference between our booths, but we became fast friends.

After I delivered my presentation to a room full of conference participants, a gentleman approached me. "Hello, I'm GG. I liked what you did. Really moving and an emotional story. I'm an agent and own the GG Greg agency," he said as he extended his hand to me. I shook his hand and said, "Nice to meet you, thank you. I am glad you enjoyed it." I was hoping his next words would be "I'd like to represent you." Instead he looked at me said, with a smile, "Get more experience and maybe we can work together in the future." I was grateful for his advice and thrilled that I just had to get more experience, but as my father would often say, "How do you get more experience if you don't hire me?"

I had to start somewhere. I made some contacts but was disappointed that I did not get any bookings, especially since I put everything on a credit card. I learned a lot from being on the other side of the table as a performer though, so the experience was really quite valuable.

I returned to Fuddruckers and the joys of morning prep, burger flipping and slamming dishes in the back as my debt increased. I was still performing comedy and still grinding, trying to make that work, along with trying to book *The Magic of Life* programs. My "office phone" was in the bakery of the restaurant. I would call Tommy throughout the day to see if we had any gigs. He would often drive to wherever we could get stage time. We took a "Comedy 101 Workshop" from local comedy legend Mike Venneman. We mostly learned how to write jokes better which really helped when you're just starting out. Everyone in the class soaked up all of Mike's advice so we could be better at our craft. It wasn't a class on "how to be funny" because honestly you can't teach that. It was a class of strengthening our material and how to be a better performer. Our "graduation" was held at Hilarities where we performed our new material from class.

Mike was an awesome mentor. He would have some of us new comedians open for him and he would pop into the club to see how we were progressing. Tommy and I also took a workshop from Dave Schwensen who once managed the infamous Improv Comedy Clubs. He focused on writing material but also the business side of comedy. That "graduation" was held at the Cleveland Improv where we performed. There was one guy in the class who, on the first day, said, "He wanted to be the funniest person in the world." He never showed up to perform.

Despite these great learning experiences, I was still in a lot of debt and my comedy/speaking career wasn't taking off as quickly as I hoped it would. I even had to ask my Dad and Dolly for money which was tough because I know they didn't have a lot to spare. In late summer of 1997, I found myself on the balcony of my fifteenth floor once again in great despair. But I remembered the dream of my mother from a couple of years earlier and backed off that ledge. Dolly, always the optimist told me, "Things will get better. You just have to believe it." When Dolly is right, Dolly is right.

One day while reading the classifieds in the Akron Beacon Journal, I saw a position at Cleveland State University for an academic adviser that also worked with orientation. Well, hell, I could do that job! It wasn't student leadership, but it would allow me to work in orientation which was something I enjoyed in grad school. I mailed my resume and secured an interview. As fate would have it, my supervisor, Sandra, from graduate school was now working at CSU in another department. She was able to be one of my references.

I interviewed in October wearing a Florida Marlins tie just after they beat the Cleveland Indians in the World Series. I figured it would be an interesting icebreaker during the interview. The advising office was hiring professional advisers moving away from their student advisors which they had been using for years. The position had a real paycheck, health care and retirement plan along with 8 a.m. to 5 p.m. hours which still allowed me my nights and weekends free to do comedy.

Fortunately, my rent was still cheap, my car was almost paid off. I could finally start paying off my debt. I got the job in December 1997. Dolly was right, things did get better.

The drive from Akron to Cleveland reminded me of the drive from Miami to North Miami Beach but with snow. Sometimes it took forty-five minutes, sometimes it took two hours. And sometimes, the drive was the best part of the day.

Academic advising in theory is not difficult, but there are people who make it harder than it has to be. I also taught the freshman orientation course, which I also did in graduate school. I was now part of a team that advised freshman students, and while it wasn't what I did in graduate school, the interaction with the students, for the most part was positive. I was able to assist with the development of orientation which I really enjoyed as well.

With normal work hours, I was still able to perform comedy. I scored some one – nighters, ranging anywhere from thirty minutes to two hours away. I was also able to create my own website for *The Magic of Life* which was a great learning experience. I still have no idea how to use html coding and would rather bang my head against the wall.

David Schwensen, whose comedy workshop I took earlier, started to manage me for *The Magic of Life*. I presented at another student activities conference in Peoria, Illinois and this time secured a couple of bookings. David and I ended up doing a double bill at Bowling Green State University, the same place where I swam my last race.

Due to not lowering my debt fast enough, I entered debt counseling, which was a huge relief, because I didn't want to declare bankruptcy. I put myself in debt and it was my responsibility to get out of it. The student loan payments were deferred once again which just meant I would be paying from the grave like any other college student.

Leadership in my office at Cleveland State was changing and I wasn't too happy with the direction. Out of curiosity, I started to look for other jobs.

On President's Day in 2000, I found an ad for an academic advising position at Kent State University. It was my day off, but I drove up to the office to work on my resume. It would be a lateral move, but with a bit more money. Plus, Kent State was only fifteen miles from my place, which would help with my commute. I was extremely excited to secure an interview for the position later in February.

It was perhaps the most fun and relaxed interview I had ever been on. At the end of my interview, Dr. Kuhn, the Dean of the department took my picture with a Polaroid camera which I thought was strange, but comical. The other gentleman in the interview was Dr. Gary Padak. Gary was a Buffalo Bills fan and we naturally 'trashed talked" a little bit since I was a huge Miami Dolphins fan. The people in the office genuinely got along and it showed in their interactions. It was a much different environment than Cleveland State and I thought I would really fit in nicely with this group. I felt pretty confident that I got the job but had to wait through the wonderful hiring process. I know HR departments do good things, but they certainly dragged their feet in this situation. I was thrilled when I finally got the offer and happily wrote my resignation letter for my position at Cleveland State University.

My inexpensive small one-bedroom apartment was now a little over $400, but due to my finances, still affordable. Technically I should have moved out of there after graduate school but was happy to still have it as my home. I was closer to work and still only a few miles from the comedy club. I didn't have to give up a thing with the new job. I was eager to start working at Kent State University. I knew the change was going to be good for me. Little did I know how working at the university would change my life and the future of *The Magic of Life* program.

Chapter 20

Turning Thirty with a Kidney Stone

In late May 2000, I quickly assimilated with my new colleagues at Kent State in the Student Advising Center. The students co-taught the orientation class for freshmen. That was the class that freshmen think they don't need because they know *everything* about college already. Helping with their training brought me back to my graduate school days. It was enjoyable to be doing that again. I was also able to secure a spot in the Student Success Series to present *The Magic of Life* as one of the many choices' students could pick for their orientation course. Not only did I have a new job, but also, I had support in presenting the program on campus.

When the evaluations came back for the program, it scored the highest marks of all the programs offered, which was a great feeling. It wasn't the same boring alcohol awareness program that the students had become accustomed to. Presenting at Kent gave me stage time, just like the comedy club, to work on *The Magic of Life* program. I was extremely grateful for the opportunity to present the program on campus and it helped get some bookings at other places as well.

A couple of months later, Big John who was now working at The University of Albany as their assistant equipment manager, quit, and became the head equipment manager position at Kent State University. We were both thrilled. He would be coming back to Ohio *and* working at the same place. The only issue was that John did not have a place to stay right away, so he stayed with me in my small apartment on the fifteenth floor. It was great. We would enjoy watching sports together; and the occasional entertaining police chase from the balcony.

Big John, being the friendly hairy giant, always left the bathtub clogged. I tried to make sure I showered first so I wouldn't have to stand in it after him. The aftermath felt like seaweed brushing against your feet in the ocean. One time, he even stepped on Mickey and didn't even realize it. That poor bird! John slept on the futon until he found his own place several blocks from campus a few months later. I thought his snoring in college was bad, but when we were under one roof, I couldn't escape it. While I missed seeing him every day, I was glad to have my apartment all to myself again.

Not long after John moved out in July of 2000, I ended up getting a kidney stone, which I believe, was a direct result of eating at Fuddruckers for two years. The first person I called was John asking him to take me to the hospital that night. But I didn't know exactly what was going on. I told him we should see how I was in the morning. If you never had a kidney stone before, let me tell you how bad it hurts—I'm Jewish and I was praying to Jesus to make the pain go away! I loved how the doctor told me to drink plenty of water. He told me to urinate in a paper strainer as if I was in the Old West looking for gold. Sadly, I didn't pass mine. It got stuck and after a few days of trying to pass it, I needed surgery. I was happy that my Dad flew up for it.

I felt bad for my father who had to sleep on the futon mattress after it was crushed by Big John. I am sure he was thrilled to be reunited with Mickey and Sunny after being apart for so long. At least he could say, "Dirty Bird" to Mickey once again. I was grateful to have my Dad there. He took care of me and "fixed" things in my apartment. He saw things that were "fire hazards" in his eyes like an extension cord under a piece of carpet. He made a long extension cord and put it around the door frame. He also bought little paint brushes for me to dust off my KISS bobbleheads. How thoughtful!

When the doctor explained the operation, he used two words in the same sentence that no man should ever hear, "penis and laser." But I didn't care I wanted the kidney stone out! I was not prepared to be wheeled into the operating room and hear the nurse say, "Michael, put your feet up in the stirrups." What? Am I giving birth now? I am happy to report that surgery was a success and I was free of that stupid kidney stone.

I spent one more year in my high-rise apartment, bringing my total tenure there to eight years. In August 2001 I moved out. With this life change came another surgery, the removal of my gallbladder. My dad flew back up from Florida to care for me once again. I am convinced the nearly 300 gallstones were also courtesy of Fuddruckers, as well. As my torso turned a nice shade of purple after the operation, something the doctor failed to inform me about, I went car shopping with my dad.

Instead of having him negotiate with the car salesman, I wanted to make him proud and I stepped up to the plate. I befriended the salesman on several visits previously. My dad was shocked when the salesman handed me the keys for the test drive and said, "come back whenever." My father looked at him with disbelief and said, "In Miami you would never see that car again."

So, despite my second surgery in a year I had a new home, a new car and one less body part. Life was going fairly well until September 11th, 2001.

I remember watching the towers fall on television. I was sitting in the residence hall next to our office. As you know, it changed so much in this country, especially air travel. Believe it or not, it impacted some of the magic tricks I was still doing in my program. I could no longer pack my needle for the "needle thru balloon" trick in my carry-on. It was deemed a weapon. I also used slush powder for a trick and since it was white, TSA would pull me out of line to investigate every time. Is it anthrax? Is it dangerous? They would ask while snapping on their blue rubber gloves, casting a suspicious glance in my direction. I didn't need to go through that ordeal every time I flew.

For years I closed my program with a "disappearing water trick." However, it seemed that people just wanted to know how I did the trick and not talk about anything else I said in the hour leading up to it. I closed the program by saying, "Without alcohol, we can live. But water, water is our life line, we need it to survive." I would pour water into an empty cup and say, "Live your life smart, make the right decisions before life disappears on you." Then I would turn the cup over, and the water would disappear! Brilliant, right?

Well traveling with the magic tricks was becoming a hassle, so like any decent performer, I evolved. I went from taping key words on the floor like a band set list to dumping the magic with the exception of the disappearing water trick. The water trick seemed corny, but the audience enjoyed it. I replaced most of the magic with comedy and I loved it. I relished the opportunity to begin each program with comedy now and it made it fun for me. The program was really making a difference and the students continually ranked it the best orientation program at Kent State; which made me happy.

Unfortunately, life at Kent changed. John was fired in 2002. It was a devastating blow for him. I didn't know all his struggles. I am sure his pride was damaged, but I did learn he worked at McDonalds for a while. It reminded me of my time at Fuddruckers, but I never gave him the grief he gave me. I knew what it was like to be in that position. He fell on hard times and eventually moved back in with his childhood friend Paul on the west side of Cleveland.

On Memorial Day weekend of 2003, Sean was next of the Six-Pack to get married. Big John had the honor of being his best man out in Seattle. Bryan and Brent were unable to make it, so John, Dennis and myself represented our little gang. We had a lot of fun that weekend and made some incredible memories with Big John serving as the source of much of the entertainment. At one local establishment, the bathroom was down a long hallway. John found a security camera and proceeded to do flips down the dingy hallway. The feed to the camera played on a little TV above the bar and soon the entire bar was watching this giant man doing somersaults. For a man of his size, he was quite spry.

I didn't see much of John after he returned to Lakewood. Life just continued for the both of us, but we would speak often. He showed up on my birthday at Hilarities in Cleveland where I was performing that night. It was good to see him again. He looked happy and was planning on going back to school for landscape architecture. As we hugged and said good-bye to each other that night, I had no idea just how much life would change in a matter of months.

Chapter 21

Big John Kelly

I know how fortunate I am to be alive. Any day I wake up, that is my best day. I'd have to say other than September 19, 1970, my worst day was May 1, 2004. It was 8:30 a.m. when the phone rang on a sunny Northeast Ohio day. I live in Northeast Ohio, so we tend to remember when the sun shines around here. My college friend and one of John's many roommates, Andy Shockney was on the other end of the line.

"Hey Gershe, it's Andy. Big John was in a fatal car accident last night," he said.

I heard the words, but I didn't quite comprehend them. "Andy, what are you talking about?"

He repeated, "Gershe, Big John was in a fatal car accident."

I was already in the denial stage of grief according to author Elisabeth Kubler-Ross's "5 stages of grief" because I did not believe what I just heard. I sat down on the arm of the couch and repeated, "Andy, what are you talking about?"

He patiently answered me a third time, "Gershe, Big John was in a fatal car accident."

My friends call me Gershe in case you were wondering why he didn't say Michael. It's rare that someone who knows me calls me by my first name.

The last time I talked with Big John it was during the NFL draft the week prior to May 1st. He called me right after his beloved Cleveland Browns selected Kellen Winslow, Jr. out of the University of Miami. I heard his big booming voice, "I DON'T WANT THAT FUCKING SOLDIER ON MY TEAM!! I HATE HIM! FUCK THAT GUY!"

John was a huge Ohio State Buckeye and Notre Dame fan, so he hated the Miami Hurricanes, which is of course, my team. In college, we would trash talk whenever our teams played each other, and it continued into adulthood. Because that is what friends do when it comes to sports.

Winslow, after losing a game in college, had a special rant where he said he was a "soldier" and anyone that hated the Canes, ridiculed and despised him for saying it. Big John was no exception.

As Andy was telling me about John, I felt numb. I slipped off the couch and onto the floor. He didn't even give me that obligatory preface of "Hey Gershe, I have something to tell you, sit down" before telling me the news. John's mom, Beverly, couldn't find my number so she contacted Andy first, thus giving him the horrible task of calling me. I hung up with Andy and sat there. I felt shocked and confused. I couldn't believe it was true so I did the only thing I could think of. I called The Bev myself. Sure enough she confirmed that her youngest of three children was killed in a car crash earlier that morning.

The mind is a weird thing because even as you're hearing the words, you're still in denial. You think you will wake up from the nightmare, but don't.

Once I hung up with John's mom, I had the responsibility of calling Brent, Dennis, Bryan, Sean and whomever else I had numbers for who knew him. I called my Dad and Dolly first for some words of comfort. Words that I desperately needed at that moment. As I dialed home, I remembered that John had teased Dolly over the years that he would come down and paint the house.

"Oh no, am so sorry to hear, he was so full of life. Such a good guy. I am so sorry Michael," Dolly said.

My Dad was just as shocked as Dolly, "That's horrible, my condolences to you, the guys and his mom. I know how close all of you were, hang in there. We will be here if you need us."

Now, the circumstances of his car crash still perplex me because John knew my story for fifteen years. He knew I presented *The Magic of Life* but never in my wildest dreams did I think a friend of mine would die as the result *of being a drunk driver*. I really thought my story would have prevented that from happening.

On his fatal night, John started at the Winking Lizard on Detroit Avenue just west of Cleveland. He ended up at Johnny Malloy's, another restaurant, on the same street. According to the press release, "a witness phoned police shortly after 2 a.m., saying he thought a 'highly intoxicated man' was in his truck." In fact, it turned out to be a different customer who saw John get into his truck. No one from the bar tried to stop him. This person gave a description of John's truck. Minutes later the police witnessed him driving.

As the police were in the process of pulling him over on a side street, blocks away from his house, he lost control of his truck, went over the curb and hit a tree head on. He was not wearing his seat belt and officers said he was going about 25-30 mph. The Lakewood Fire Department was called to the scene and began CPR. John died shortly after being transported to the hospital. He suffered from multiple injuries to his head, neck, chest and abdomen. This was the first traffic fatality in the city in about two years.

One of my best friends died as a result of being a drunk driver and it rattled every part of me. He knew better. He knew better and yet, I felt that I failed him. This would have been John's first DUI and I wonder how many times he drove drunk prior to his death. I can't vilify my friend, but how ironic that my mother died at the hands of a drunk driver and John died as a drunk driver? Alcohol was the common denominator. As I sat in my apartment, I found myself screaming at him.

The first call I made to the Six-Pack was Bryan and with a lump in my throat, I began with, "Hey Bryan, are you sitting down? Sit down, I have something to tell you." That's how I began all the phone calls.

Bryan wanted me to come down to his house about ninety minutes away, but I was so paralyzed, there was no way I could drive. I was just trying to breathe.

I asked Bryan if he would call Dennis, but he declined. Gee, thanks buddy. Ugh.

As I dialed Dennis' number, I felt numb. "Hey Dennis, are you sitting down?"

You never forget those calls. With some things in life, repetition makes things easier. Telling your friends that one of your best friends is dead was not one of them.

The reactions were all the same - "How?" "What?" "Why" and tears flowed. Now I knew how Andy felt when he called me. Calling Bryan, Brent and Dennis was agonizing, but I was now faced with extremely difficult task of calling Sean out in Seattle where it was close to 6:30 in the morning.

John and Sean shared a tight bond. They were two peas in a pod. I never saw two people eat like them in my life. Plus, remember, John, was Sean's best man at his wedding less than a year ago. As I slowly dialed Sean's number, I thought about how I would rather have another kidney stone than go through with this phone call and break the news to Sean.

I struggled getting the words out, just like I did with the previous phone calls. As I fought back my tears I said, "Sean, we lost Big John. Big John died, we lost Big John."

I could hear his wife at the time, Heather, saying, "Sean, what's wrong?" over his tears through the phone.

"Once I heard the phone ring, I knew something bad happened," Sean said between sobs. It was so painful. God, why couldn't Bryan or Dennis or Brent make this call, why me? So many questions had to be answered. For one, how on earth do you comfort someone on the opposite coast through the telephone when all you want to do is give them a huge hug? The deaths of my mother, grandmother and grandfather were one thing, but this was so different. We were thirty-three and trying to come to grips with the fact that one of our best friends, someone that we have known since we were eighteen and nineteen-years-old, was now dead.

John was in college for six years and everybody who crossed paths with him loved him. I remember having to call information to find people's numbers if I didn't have them. It felt like my apartment was the central hub for information, and to be honest, it kept me so busy that I never started the grieving process. I was too busy being there for everyone else that I didn't take time to process the day. That night, I ended up meeting another longtime friend, Matt, who worked as John's assistant at Kent for dinner at Damon's Bar and Grill.

We headed to the bar as we waited for our table and ordered two tallboys of Coors Light. It was John's favorite. We made a toast to our friend and quickly downed the beer. We ordered two more and while Matt drank his, I stared at mine, watching the condensation drip down the glass.

At that moment, it finally hit me that Big John was dead. I could have drunk ten of those tallboys that night and it wouldn't have solved the issues that were stirring deep inside of me. One of my best friends was dead, and he died as a drunk driver. I left my second beer at the bar.

Neither one of us felt like eating, but we slowly made our way through the meal trying to make sense of it all.

When I got home from dinner, I was unable to sleep or sit still. I started to scan pictures that would be a part of a tribute video I wanted to show at his funeral. As I went through my photo albums, I found a picture of John and me from my graduation where I sat on his shoulders like a little kid. Another favorite was one from Brent's wedding, which turned out, was the last time all six of us were together. We looked so dapper and dare I say, "good looking studs" in our tuxedos under the full moon. I focused on finding whatever pictures I had of John and put together a video of memories to a few songs.

My plan was to create a video with two of his favorite songs, *Best of Times* by Styx and *Piano Man* by Billy Joel. I distracted myself from sleeping, eating and processing his death by working on the video. It was the only thing that kept me sane. At least I was finally putting my television minor to good use with the editing! I did anything I could to avoid grieving for my friend. When someone asked me how I was doing, I replied with the obligatory, "I'm fine."

Since John worked at Kent State University for a few years, my co-workers knew him pretty well. John was a part of our lunch gang where the laughs never stopped. I mustered the energy to go into the office the next day so I could put an away message on my both phone and email. I didn't even have to ask for the time off, it was pretty much, "come back when you're ready."

Gary, my supervisor, who, along with me, would harass John along with me at Kent's home football games, offered his support like everyone. They were in shock over his death too. I couldn't have asked for better people to work with during this difficult time. Not having to worry about work was a huge relief.

The Bev and I talked quite frequently during that week about the wake and funeral. The Six-Pack along with a few other of John's friends, including Andy and Matt were pall bearers. With John being 6'4 and close to 300 pounds at the time of his death, the more bodies we had, the better. If everyone that knew John, and wanted to, could have a hand on that coffin, we would have made it possible. In planning the memorial service, The Bev asked me how much food to get, "Gershe, enough for twenty to thirty people?" I told her, "Mrs. Kelly, your son was at Ashland for six years, he was loved by a lot of people. We will need a lot more food." Even the college president once celebrated New Years with John at the "BK House." John was the glue that held our little Ashland community together.

Big John Kelly graduating from Ashland University

Chapter 22

A Big Farewell

We stayed in touch, and would visit each other, but the last time the six of us were together was Brent's wedding ten years ago. Now we were coming together for Big John's funeral. We all thought we would grow old together and continue to insult each other well into our senior years. Brent said that he could not get the time off from the Army to come back for the wake and funeral which was disappointing. But somehow his wife, Karan was able to work her magic and they were both able to come back to Ohio for John.

Dennis was flying in from New Jersey and his arrival time happened to be at the same time KISS tickets were going on sale. I started to panic because even though I love Dennis as a brother, I had to get decent seats for KISS. Surely he would understand if I was late. Bryan said, "Relax, I can get Dennis." It was one less thing I had to take care of. I was running on fumes and wanted the video to be perfect. I was determined to match up certain pictures with the lyrics and obsessed over every little detail.

Sean and his wife were flying into Columbus from Seattle to stay with his mom. As if I wasn't stressed enough, the day of the wake, he was running late, two hours away.

There were two viewings. I wanted to be there for both of them, but I waited for Andy and Sean to show up. With Dennis, Brent and Bryan already at my apartment, the wait was pure torture. I just wanted to get there and see John. Not just see him, but be with him. Sean and Andy were worth the wait. A wake or funeral is not the occasion I wanted to reunite with my friends but seeing them was comforting. After many hugs and some laughs, we made our way to see our Big John.

When we got the funeral home, I didn't know what to expect in terms of who would be there. I was just hoping to keep it together. As we walked in, I saw several people from college that I hadn't seen in years. I saw Shrubber and gave him a long embrace as we consoled each other. Then, I got in "the line" to see John.

This is the line that no one wants to be in because it's filled with unsettling anticipation. A week ago, I was just talking with him and now, I would see one of my best friends in a coffin. My palms were sweaty as my stomach turned, and I wished I was anywhere but here. John, Sean, Dennis, Brent, Bryan and I were a little gang of immature, fun-loving guys that everyone knew. As I stood in that dreadful line, all I could think about was the times we shared and how I really didn't want to see him like this. He was so full of life.

As I looked down at John laying in his purple Ashland University orientation jacket, I didn't hear a sound around me. I studied his face, and how the make-up looked in the light. I was screaming inside seeing him like this and I didn't want to leave his side, but knew people were behind me.

I quickly walked outside to get some air. I felt like I was suffocating. I slumped down onto a step, paralyzed with emotion and stared off in disbelief that Big John was gone. I was in my own little world when I felt Sean's presence near me.

He said, "Hey bud, you are doing alright?"

I nodded and "Yeah, I am okay."

I was the furthest thing from being "okay."

We headed back inside where I finally found John's mom, sister and brother. We consoled each other and talked for a while. I made my way through the crowd, catching up with old college friends. Again, I wished I was anywhere but here. The line to view John dissipated and I went back to see him.

Standing there was another college roommate of his, Melissa. I just stood silently next to her as we stared upon our friend.

She broke the silence by saying, "He looks like he is sleeping."

I replied, without missing a beat, "Yeah, but he would be snoring."

She laughed, and I finally felt human again by making her laugh, even if it did only last for a few seconds.

The wake concluded. Paul, his childhood friend and current roommate, invited us back to his house. As I was leaving the funeral home, I walked past a room where the door was ajar. Inside that room was John's older brother, Tim, sitting alone with his hands clasped and his head down. I paused for a few seconds, contemplating going in to sit next to him. Maybe my presence would be helpful. But I froze, because I knew if I walked into the room, there was nothing I could say that would make things better. The image of Tim in that room has stuck with me over the years.

It was so powerful. Death, especially sudden death like John's, changed us all because he was always the life of the party. He was the guy that had the goofy grin that could light up the room. His booming voice and laughter would fill the air with such pleasure. Then again, the stench of his feet would do the exact opposite! Seeing Tim in those few seconds made me think of all the things we would miss about Big John Kelly.

About twenty of us gathered in Paul's house after the wake for food and trips down memory lane. There were tears and laughter as we remembered our friend. With the funeral two days away, I was still trying to find people that knew John. In the midst of a kitchen full of people, I was still locating friends telling them about Big John. What a shitty way to reconnect with people that you haven't talked to or seen in years. The calls were still so brutal, and I was numb from all of them.

John was a prolific photographer. He captured many of our memories. Unbeknownst to anyone else, he was busy organizing his pictures, either via scanning them or in shoe boxes. His sister Therese thought I had organized them all. She was just as surprised as anyone that he was the one who did it. I mean John was not the most organized guy in the world. When he moved to Kent after living in my tiny apartment, he really didn't have money for curtains or blinds, so he nailed up a sheet up instead to cover his sliding glass door. It was hysterical and yet typical John. You would walk into his apartment and couldn't see the carpet under a sea of his clothes. There was one time when the only thing hanging up in his closet on a single hanger was a windbreaker. Everything else was on the floor.

Another story I love sharing about John ,which I've included in my program over the years, is that he would never lock his car door. On some mornings, I would drive by his place, move his car seat all the way up and then head to my office. Can you guess what happens when someone of his stature tries to get into a car with the seat inches from the steering wheel? It would piss him off, but I could never stop laughing when he would show up in my office swearing at me. These were the memories we now shared with each other to pass the time before the funeral.

My temporary roommates and I headed back to my place. I enjoyed having my apartment full of my friends despite it being for a horrible reason. It was a great escape, granted, I believe I got the brunt of the verbal abuse. I tried to tune them out as I worked on the tribute video. Dennis said he was sick of hearing the Styx song, but I needed that video to be perfect. The night before the funeral, five of us stayed in my one- bedroom apartment with a loft. I was happy that Dolly forced me to get that sofa bed when I first moved in. I offered the futon to Dennis, but he happily slept under the stairs. In the morning, I got donuts and juice. It was going to be a long day for everyone. No one made much conversation as we quietly prepared for what would be an emotional day.

The anticipation of the funeral was mounting as butterflies flew around in my stomach. I barely spoke a full sentence at my grandfather's burial and now I had to give my first eulogy. Sure, I had experience as a comedian and speaker, but this was totally different. As we headed back to the funeral home for the last viewing, before the service, I realized I left the video that I'd been working on day and night at home. Thankfully, we were only two miles away, but I needed that video since I really had no idea what else I would do or say during the memorial service.

We had the opportunity to view John one last time before we brought him to the church. The reality of his death finally hit me as I stood before him, saying my goodbye.

I somberly walked out of the room. Suddenly every ounce of emotion that had been building up all week purged out of my body as I started to drop to the floor. Brent turned around and caught me. I felt completely exhausted and drained. I was trying to be strong for everyone else. I needed the help. Brent and I walked outside joining the other pallbearers. I hugged Bryan and felt the tears flow as I used his shoulder as a tissue. We patiently waited for the funeral director to wheel John out as we stared at each other in silence. As we gripped his coffin, someone said, "One, two, three, LIFT!" It created some much-needed laughter as we put him into the hearse.

When we got to the church, we continued our responsibility and honor of bringing John in. As we wheeled him slowly, the hallway of the church was lined with family and friends. I wanted to stop the procession and give people hugs but we continued to push him into the sanctuary for the service. I sat between Bryan and Dennis in the front row as the service began. Halfway through, Dennis was playing with his program and dropped it onto the floor. Bryan and I stared at him like parents of a disobedient child. As he reached down slowly to pick it up, he flashed us one of his trademark smiles which made us shake our heads with a slight chuckle. Good tension breaker, maybe not the best time or place, but it helped!

When the religious ceremony was over, we all gathered in the basement for lunch and the memorial service. Matt and I really had no plan other than showing the video as people ate and talked among themselves. I had years of experience as a comedian and speaker, but I was clueless about what I would say. I didn't want to sound like a babbling idiot filled with emotion but wanted to make sure we honored John correctly. I do know that John wouldn't want us to be all sad and would want us to be celebrating in some fashion. I just used what always worked for me in any other stressful situation—humor.

As I got everyone's attention and introduced both Matt and me, I said, "By a show of hands how many people fed Big John before?" A sea of hands went up in the air along with a lot of smiles. "How many of you fed him and even though he said, 'I'll pay you back' you knew he never would but did it just for his company?" Again, hands went up with some laughter and more smiles.

I thought to myself, "Good, we are starting to feel human again."

I introduced the video and hoped people would enjoy it. The tribute played on the old nineteen-inch TV and cut his head off in some of the pictures. He was even too big for the television.

After the video I confessed to his mom that a reason why it may have taken him six years to graduate was because I would turn off his alarm a lot during his freshman year. That got more laughs. My voice started to quiver as I promised his mom, "That as long as I do my program, every audience will know your son."

No matter where he went, people knew and loved her son and I would make sure people still did.

Matt gave his eulogy and then I thought it would be a good idea to see if others wanted to say anything. Now, at this particular moment, I thought it was a *great* idea, not realizing how difficult it would be for people. I just wanted others to be able to share what John meant to them. I nudged Dennis a little bit to speak, and once he started, I realized it was a horrible idea because it was just too hard for him.

A few people did speak, and it was a lovely way to memorialize Big John.

The last person to speak was John's mom who thanked everyone for coming and remembering her son. I don't think she really understood the impact that John had on so many people. He was loved by so many because he gave everyone a bit of his heart and soul. He was one of the kindest people you could ever have the pleasure of knowing in life. As things were winding down, Brent,

Bryan, Dennis, Sean and I took a picture with his mom before we all departed.

John had a way of bringing people together, but his funeral was not the way it was supposed to be. The five remaining members of our little Six-Pack walked through the church parking lot slowly. We laughed and resorted back to our college days when we gave each other the finger or slapped each other on the forehead. It didn't matter if we were in the church parking lot, we had just been through hell. As we were saying our heartfelt goodbyes, I saw Brent hug Sean. It was such a tender moment between two brothers before Brent, being, well, Brent, smacked Sean in the groin just like he would do in college. Bryan and I just shook our heads and laughed as Sean doubled over in pain while Brent busted out laughing. Somewhere, we knew, our friend Big John Kelly was laughing as well.

The Bev asked me to join the family for a private burial a couple of weeks later, but my brother and I were already booked for a cruise. John was cremated and would be laid to rest in the same plot as his father. John's name would eventually be added to the headstone. As I joined my brother onto the ship, part of me was back in Ohio, as they buried John.

It was my first cruise and I thought it would be the perfect escape from everything. My Dad and Dolly dropped us off at the Port of Miami and then proceeded to watch us leave while sitting in chairs across the channel. It felt like we were little kids again, but it was pretty cool to see them wave at us as we left port. I didn't have to worry about driving so Jeff kept on feeding me Bahama Mama's. I might have had four or five before we even left port. I figured I could drink a bit to drown my sorrows without the responsibility of driving. Besides, if the Captain asked me to steer the ship, then I knew we were all in trouble. As we left port, Jeff asked, "So how do you like cruising?" I was loving it and we were just getting started.

When I got back to Ohio after the cruise, I called The Bev to see how she was doing and to find out John's location in the cemetery. She asked if I had a good time on the cruise in which I replied, "Yes. I can't wait to do it again." Then she asked me a question that I never would have imagined. She said, "So, did you meet anyone on the ship?" I laughed and paused because here was a devout Catholic woman asking me if I "hooked up" with anyone on the four-day trip. It wasn't my goal when I got on the ship and so unlike me to do so, but I said, "Yes I did Mrs. Kelly. Yes, I did. But I didn't do it for me, I did it for Big John!" She let out a huge laugh and said, "Oh good, he would have appreciated that!

Top from left: Brent, Dennis, Bryan, Matt
Bottom from left: Me, The Bev, Sean

Chapter 23

Life after Big John

We all struggled after the death of Big John as we tried to resume our lives. When we thought about him, we laughed and cried at the same time. We organized a golf outing and bowling event where we raised money for a scholarship in his name at Ashland University. Plus, it was another chance for all of us to get together in his honor. I made an updated video using pictures that John's mom gave me. I loved seeing his baby pictures and him as a kid but was saddened that my friend was gone.

When we all parted from that church parking lot, we relied on each other for support as best as we could through phone calls and emails. Continuing day to day meant coping with John's death. On one of my doctor visits I mentioned that I was a little depressed and he gave me some tips to cope. I tried, but it still wasn't quite enough. One of his suggestions was to sit in the sun and feel its warmth. Great advice doc, but I live in Northeast Ohio, we don't see the sun for days at a time around here. There was a psychiatrist office on the 2nd floor of the medical building, and after some procrastinating, I made an appointment. It was the first time I would be talking about grief to anyone. As we talked about John, the psychiatrist said I had "situational depression" and only felt that way because John's death was so recent.

I only went a couple of times to see the counselor. I thought, like a typical male, well, it's only situational depression, I will be just fine. Let me just stop thinking about what reminds me of my friend, which was nearly impossible. Going to work reminded me of John. Sometimes, I would drive by his old apartment and sit in the parking lot looking at the sliding glass door expecting to see that sheet he nailed up as a curtain.

Looking back now, I wasn't fully ready to open up to anyone about how John's death affected me. I did what my father did, stayed quiet and pushed my grief aside.

As I prepared to give three programs in a row for Kent State's freshmen for the fall semester, I fulfilled my promise to John's mom by including him in *The Magic of Life*. I started my program to honor my mother and to make sure others didn't go through what my family did. I had to speak about John now, because here was a guy that knew my story and yet, it didn't stop him. Now, I was speaking for his family and friends. I would do whatever I could to prevent others from being the next Big John. I was already doing the program, so who better than me to do it?

I loved Big John like a brother, but I hated him for making me take on this responsibility of sharing his story. I hated the fact I had to relive the moment I got the call from Andy and then making all the calls to the Six-Pack. As much as I hated it, I also knew there was no one better to deliver the message.

When Freshman Orientation arrived, Bryan came for emotional support which I desperately needed. Since I have no memories of my mother, talking about her is slightly easier than talking about John. I am not saying it's easy by any means, but I had known Big John for fifteen years. There are a lot of memories in those years.

I thought the lump in my throat would prevent me from talking about him. When the time came in the program to talk about Big John, I put his graduation picture up on the screen. It was one of his proudest moments. I wanted the audience to see the infectious smile that everybody who knew him knew.

I felt the tears start to roll down my face. My brain knew the words, but my mouth had trouble saying them. It may seem odd, but I felt his presence with me during those three programs. Somehow and perhaps with the guidance of John, I pushed through it. And as I promised his mom months earlier, people now knew her son.

John's death really impacted me in ways I hadn't considered. I started to look for other opportunities in life. In fall of 2004, I applied for another job on campus in a different department. It was a step up from my current level. I had also applied for the Director of Orientation position at Florida Gulf Coast University. If I got that job, it would put me two hours away from my family which was a great thought.

I also thought more about *The Magic of Life* and how it was growing. I was grateful to have the opportunity at Kent to fine tune it every year and that helped me when I was booked at other universities or high schools. In the back of mind, I wondered, "Can I do this full time?" I attended another college activities conference which kept me motivated in presenting the program. Like in the past ones I attended, I would chat with a few agents, such as GG Greg who I met years before.

In December of 2004, I accepted the position at Kent with a little more money and a new title. I also landed an interview at FGCU for the other job. I was in a slight quandary between the two of them. With my mental state still dealing with John, felt I should take the interview to see my options. I had also sent my promo package to a popular college agency, Coleman Productions, because I thought, "Well, it's time to stop putting it on the back burner. You have to see if this thing has legs." The agency was owned by successful speaker, David Coleman, who was at the top of the college market. He was who I aspired to be.

During the interview at Florida Gulf Coast, they asked how many programs I did a year. At that time, I was doing about ten. But when the person asked, it really made me think of what I wanted. I was offered the job unofficially at the end of the interview which was a great feeling. When I got back to Ohio, I found out that the agency was interested in my program too, and I could join their rosters of speakers. I was ecstatic! I had some big decisions to make.

The money situation at FGCU just wasn't going to work out since the cost of living in the Naples area was much higher than where I lived in Ohio. I reluctantly turned down the job. Besides I just took a new position at Kent and was thrilled about signing with a college agent. I thought, "This is it; my career is going to take off!" All my hard work was paying off with the program. This was my goal. I had saved up enough money from previous programs for the agency's "buy in" and then hoped I would make that money back.

I soon realized I wasn't like a lot of other speakers, and alcohol wasn't considered a "hot" topic. People admitted that it was a problem on campus, but booking it was another issue. I just didn't understand that if it was a concern, then why not book the program? We are trying to save lives with my program. I was able to do four or five programs my first year with the agency and a few more in 2006.

I was just one of many faces on the roster with some of them speaking for a lot longer than me on different topics. I was spending money at conferences with the hope of recouping it by getting booked, but that wasn't the case.

In December of 2006, the agency let me go and brought on another alcohol speaker with whom they had a longer relationship with. It really hurt me because I felt they already had me, why not work with me more? Not to knock the other speaker because he had a powerful story too, but I thought I was better. It also taught me a valuable lesson that if I was going to make it, I was going to make it on my own merits not on someone else's coattails. Getting dumped by that agency was a blessing in disguise because David, the agency owner, and I eventually became close friends, which has been wonderful. I could have stayed mad, but it gave me a reason to call GG Greg who told me all those years ago, "Get more experience."

I called GG and explained to him what happened. Since we kept in touch over the years, he knew that I had gained more experience. We talked about my goals for the program and we were committed to saving lives together.

It's pretty amazing to look back now and see how all my decisions in life led me to this moment. Sometimes we are just busy living life to really notice how everything impacts our decisions, or where we end up in life. Maybe it is fate. But whether I was going to speak full time or part-time, I was excited for this new opportunity.

Perhaps another sign that it was time to focus on speaking is that after twenty-six years of being my pet, my friend, Mickey, that rambunctious grey cockatiel, passed away in January 2007. He was my little buddy who loved chirping to feet and would give me the wolf whistle every time I walked into my home. But he was old and kept on falling off his perch, showing signs that he was getting closer to the end. When I was on the road doing presenting *The Magic of Life*, Mickey was staying with a "pet sitter" instead of a close friend because I didn't want him to die on my friend's watch.

As I was leaving a program at Denison University and on my way to speak at a conference in Michigan, I got the call that Mickey died. Oddly enough I was presenting at the same conference as the speaker that replaced me. Truthfully, I am glad I wasn't home when Mickey died. I don't know what I would have done if I uncovered the cage in the morning only to see him at the bottom of it like I did with Sunny a couple of years earlier.

Walking into my apartment and not hearing him was quite eerie and sometimes, even after all these years, I am still not quite used to it. I saw Mickey's death as a sign that I didn't have to worry about him when I went back on the road to present *The Magic of Life*.

Mickey loved talking to himself

Chapter 24

The Magic of Life Program

There are days when I think, "Did I give up on my comedy dream too soon?" I still wanted to have my name on those table tents I saw at the comedy club back when I was a teenager. There are thousands of comedians out there and many who are a lot funnier than me. But instead of being in a sea among them, there is only one person presenting *The Magic of Life*. My purpose is not just to perform comedy, my purpose is to inspire people and prevent impaired driving.

I still perform comedy regularly, but I can present *The Magic of Life* and combine my "comedy stylings" with my story for a fun, emotional, impactful life changing event. The ability to inspire and change lives while making people laugh is the best of both worlds. The program was really named *The Magic of Life* because of the magic I was performing in it. It has evolved so much over the years, that the title now captures what the spirit of life should really be about.

From starting out with magic tricks to what it is now, I feel so lucky to be able to present the program and create a difference in society. I think it has been fascinating to look back and see how the decisions I've made led to the program. As we are making decisions in life, we don't know how things will turn out, as we just live in the moment of the journey. We all have a purpose in life and *The Magic of Life* is mine.

If I hadn't gone to Ashland, I wouldn't have gotten involved in student activities such as the campus activities board or have become a peer educator. If I didn't go to graduate school at The University of Akron, I never would have met Lucy who booked the comedians. If I didn't leave Cleveland State for Kent State, I don't think the program would be as successful as it is now.

Take a moment now and reflect on the decisions you've made in your life and how it influenced what you are doing today. I knew what I wanted to do, though, at times, I admit, I had no clue what I was doing. Nevertheless, each step got me to what I am doing today. I could have easily done nothing in my life to make a difference, but I'm damn glad I chose to do something to prevent drunk driving!

I loved the creative process as I developed *The Magic of Life* program. I enjoy taking an idea and giving it life on stage. I remember what my communications professor and adviser, Dr. Beth Richmond, told us on the first day of class, "Know your audience." Every audience I am in front of, whether it's high school students, college students, military members, or DUI offenders, is so different. I know what I have to do to reach them. No matter who they are, I want them to laugh and walk out of the program with a better understanding about life. It's quite humbling when people call me a "miracle" because I still see myself as that goofy kid from the suburbs of Miami.

In 2014, I had the honor of presenting at Minot Air Force Base for the first time. Along with presenting the program for several hundred Airmen, they gave me a special behind the scenes experience. They put me in protective gear and allowed the cute guard dog to attack me. If there was a definition of "scared shitless" in the dictionary, it would be me being chased by the cute puppy dog as if I was dinner. I also got to fly a B-52 Bomber flight simulator where I crashed somewhere in Guam. I was so grateful to not only share my program, but to see what they go through on a daily basis serving our country.

In May 2016, during my second visit to Minot Air Force Base, I was scheduled to do eight programs with no guard dogs in sight! Three of them were full length, but the others were ten-minute programs for those who had guard duty. These brave men and women were headed for a long day protecting the base and one program was to begin at 5:30 a.m.

I began the shorter program with, "I am a huge Star Wars nerd. I really want that R2D2 shower head that lights up and makes noises when you turn it on. However, I'm forty-six years old and single, I'm pretty sure if I get one of those, I'm never having sex again!" Those men and women standing in formation with their weapons laughed and it broke the ice. Heck one Airman admitted to having one! It made them forget just for a little bit how stressful their day was about to be. I enjoy making an audience laugh. It gives them a taste of my personality.

When I started talking about the car crash a few moments later, they were more vested in the discussion and really heard my story.

Being blessed with a sense of humor gives me the ability to wake up a high school audience at 7:30 a.m. Laughter allows the audience to understand that this program is different from what they thought it would be. I love making fun of high school menus which usually makes the students laugh. When one high school served applesauce nearly every day, I simply said, "You all eat more applesauce than residents at my father's assisted living facility." I had no idea if it was going to be funny, but the high school audience erupted and even applauded. They sent me tweets about it later on. Humor allows for that type of connection and it's priceless.

In most high school gyms, the clocks behind the basketball net are encased in a theft proof fence. "Who is trying to steal the clocks? If you're that bad at basketball that you're hitting the clocks behind the basket, then perhaps basketball is not for you." Using humor allows me to let the audience know, "This is not going to be same drunk driving program that you've heard before."

If I started the program with the car crash, what am I going to talk about for the next fifty-five minutes?

They have no idea who I am other than, "Well, here's a stranger who is going to talk to you for a while."

I like building up to the crash because once I make them laugh, I can take an audience anywhere on the journey.

Ever face thirty DUI offenders who would rather be *anywhere* but in that courtroom for an hour? I love watching their body language change from being defensive to acceptance during the program, because I make them laugh first. With the DUI offenders, I am not there to judge them, or talk down to them, and by using humor, it makes them feel not so ashamed of being there. They feel like a real person, not a criminal. On the surveys that we give offenders, many of them have written that they didn't expect the humor but enjoyed it because it made the program different than what they expected.

I do not believe in the "doom and gloom" approach which many school administrators like to do. They love putting on a mock drunk driving crash, a mock court hearing and mock funeral to impact their students. Let's beat the kids over the head with doom and gloom. Years ago, I spoke at a high school in New Jersey and they did the mock drunk driving crash where one of their fellow students was the drunk driver and a fellow student "died." I don't think you have to shock an audience to get them to learn and, sometimes, it's just too much.

In their auditorium, they had a mock funeral set up where they had caskets up on stage and people spoke as if students died. People were crying but, yet, everyone was alive and well. Prior to the event, a mom saw the coffins and was highly upset. "This is too much, I don't want my daughter seeing this," she told me. I calmed her down by saying, "Please let her stay for my program. I promise you it will be fun and also meaningful." She reluctantly agreed, and I was happy. What I didn't know, is that the mock funeral would be over an hour, but it felt like four! It was just painful.

When I finally took the stage and tossed out the first joke, the laughter from those students hit me like a tidal wave. They felt like themselves again and I was thrilled. Laughter is an amazing tool to use and those students hung on every word I said after that initial laugh. When I got to the serious part, they stayed with me and it was even more effective. It wasn't a mock story any more,

I was a guy who made them laugh and now told a powerful, emotional story. I've been pretty successful in getting an audience to learn by incorporating humor into the very serious topic of drunk driving. People will not pay attention when they are subjected to all that doom and gloom.

After the program, the same mother came running up to me. She gave me a huge hug and exclaimed, "That was the only thing those kids needed to hear today! Thank you for making a difference in my daughter's life!" It's quite nice when students thank me for making them laugh and for having the "courage" to share my story. I tell audiences that humor is that one natural high we all need and that won't kill us like alcohol or drugs. It is my salvation and it has helped me survive this long in life.

The irony of being a comedian is that I've spent my life making people laugh, but the one laugh I never heard was my mother's.

Many speakers who present about drunk driving like to use statistics. I do not rely heavily on stats. I'd rather give the audience a powerful, emotional message that is going to hit them in their heart. Statistics are based on things that happened in the past, and I cannot do anything about the past. The people in my audiences are sons, daughters, mothers and fathers. They are not numbers.

I do, however, show stats when presenting for DUI offenders, only to show a quick glimpse of trends in the state of Ohio. Many of them are surprised that the number are higher than they expected. I tell them, "My job is to focus on you. I can't change the past, but I can try and change your future by sharing my story. More importantly you can change your future, I can only do so much." We don't have to change alone. We can look at people in our lives who have been positive role models for inspiration.

Presenting at the Stow Municipal Court for DUI offenders

Chapter 25

Role Models

Years ago, I took a career counseling course at Kent State University taught by Dr. Mark Savickas. He has done some amazing work in the field throughout his career. During class we discussed how role models influence a person's life. It made me think of my role models, not just family members, but anyone, real or fictitious. For the past couple of years, I've included my role models into the program, because first, it's fun; and second, I want people to think about their positive influences. As I share a bit about my role models, think about yours and how they have impacted your life.

When I started to read, I got into Winnie the Pooh and I immediately gravitated toward Tigger. He was always bouncing around, making sure people were happy and laughing. I even had Tigger pajamas that I squeezed into when they were too small for me. No, I don't have them anymore. I know you were wondering. But, I do have a Tigger stuffed animal though. As a comedian, it's my job to make sure people are happy and laughing.

Tigger was just a loveable character. Though I may not be loveable and positive every day, I know he influenced me to try and stay upbeat even on the hard days. Who was your favorite Winnie the Pooh character and why? Does that character fit your personality?

When I advanced my reading skills a little bit more, I got into Spider-Man. Not only did I identify with Spidey, but also with Peter Parker. Peter is shy, quiet, into photography, lost his parents, survived the death of his Uncle Ben and was raised by his Aunt May. Off stage, I can be shy and quiet. I love photography, lost my mother, and Dolly was my Aunt May. I also had problems with girlfriends, paying rent and debt.

Like Peter, I was bullied too. In Junior High, my bully sat behind me in math class. He was a lot bigger than me and already looked like he was twenty. I was lucky to have any facial hair. This guy could grow a beard before the school day was over. He would always hit me in the back or in the head during class. I tried to ignore him, but it was pretty hard to do. Besides, the fact he outweighed me by fifty to sixty pounds, if not more. I found out he also bullied some of my other friends. I did find some solace in that he grew up to be a podiatrist. He might make more money than me, but he chose a career where he has to touch stinky and gross feet every day.

When Peter becomes Spider-Man, he uses humor as a defense mechanism to distract his enemies, similar to how I used it against bullies. I used humor in college when I was picked on for being Jewish. Humor is like a mask that hides my pain. As a hero, Spidey saves one life at a time and with my program, I try to do the same thing. His Uncle Ben told him, "With great power comes great responsibility." I believe I was kept alive and given a power, thus a responsibility to share my story to make a difference, to save lives. Throughout the years of presenting *The Magic of Life*, I know I have saved a few lives. Who is your favorite superhero and why? What do you see in yourself that you see in them?

While we are discussing literary figures, James Bond is another role model. Yes, I know, an assassin? Roger Moore was Bond when I was a kid and had that great humor element. Notice a theme so far with my role models? I enjoyed the character developed by Ian Fleming. Bond is a loner, an orphan after his parents died, and has a list of flaws that are a mile long. When I ask DUI offenders who likes Bond, many times a woman will raise her hand and say, "I like him because he's a badass and he's hot." The men will say, "He's suave, has the cool car and gadgets." When they say "suave" I reply, "Just like me!"

Bond always did what he had to do to save the day. He uses humor, like Spider-man to distract his enemies in stressful situations and despite his personal flaws, he has self-confidence to do what is right no matter the cost. I admire that in the character. He has morals and stands by them, something I identify with too.

So far, all my role models, outside my family, are fictional characters. It seems that I had quite the imaginative childhood! I loved escaping deep within those worlds and perhaps it is how I coped with the death of my mother as a kid. The one constant theme is that they used humor in their lives. How have your role models impacted your life?

While I am not against the use of alcohol, I don't want people hurting themselves or others. Peer pressure sometimes puts us in the wrong situation when alcohol or drugs are involved. I stress the importance of standing up for yourself and if you don't want to engage in alcohol or drugs, that is okay. My last two role models are Gene Simmons and Paul Stanley of KISS. They taught me a lot about facing peer pressure and standing up for yourself. I appreciate the fact that my father told me to "turn the music down," but never off, when I would blast KISS in my room while "supposedly" doing my homework. I learned a lot about life from men who wear makeup!

During this point in the program I tell the audience, "Here I am talking about standing up for yourself and being proud of who you are and I'm not even showing my true self to you. Can I show my true self to you?" When they respond with a "Yes!" I ask them to clap to get some energy in the room as the clapping gets faster, I turn around showing off my nice bald spot while removing my long-sleeved shirt. I reveal a black KISS t-shirt with the band's name on the back in huge letters and their faces on the front. In fact, I'm wearing a KISS shirt right now!

It still makes me smile to hear audience members, even middle school students, cheer when they see my

KISS shirt. I enjoy taking pictures with our military, our tongues sticking out like Gene Simmons after my program. One thing Gene and Paul taught me is if you show people your true self, no one can take that away. Be proud of who you are. I don't care if you have purple hair, or have 80 piercings in your face, if you are happy, great!

Gene Simmons and Paul Stanley never embraced alcohol or drugs, and that really resonated with me growing up. They even kicked Ace Frehley and Peter Criss out of the band due to those vices because they were ruining the band. They were also ruining Gene and Paul's dream with their addictions. Sometimes you have to kick people out of your life if they are putting you in harm's way. How many talented musicians, actors and artists have died because they used alcohol and drugs? Your dreams and goals are too important to abuse alcohol and drugs. Reflect now on your own dreams. Are they worth giving up?

I've been lucky enough to thank Gene and Paul in person for being my role models which was quite emotional for me. I gave each of them a *The Magic of Life* wristband which Gene put on as we spoke.

"What happened to the man who killed your mother?" Gene asked me.

"He was sentenced to three years with time served."

Gene shook his head in disgust and said, "I believe in vengeance. An eye for an eye."

I told him, "In my twenties I would have pulled the trigger for that vengeance."

I understand that not everyone likes Gene and that is fine. He is another flawed role model. But a role model for me and other KISS fans. Wearing the KISS shirt gives me a psychological inner strength for the next part of the program when I talk about the car crash and the death of my mother.

Without a doubt my Dad and Dolly are my role models within my family. They have both taught me about unconditional love, compassion, and what the human spirit is capable of doing. They supported my dreams and molded me into the person I am today. I am not perfect and have my flaws, but at the end of the day, I like to think I am making the right decisions in my life—for a better life. At least most of the time. I have made many mistakes in life, but they've encouraged me that "things will get better" in time. They've let me learn from my mistakes.

I implore you to thank your role models if you get that chance because it is an amazing experience. Let them know the impact they've had in your life.

Meeting Gene Simmons

Meeting
Paul
Stanley

Spent my 40th Birthday with KISS, Minot, ND 7/24/10

Chapter 26

The Joy of Making a Difference

If the focus of *The Magic of Life* is more alcohol awareness, I will do a "choices and consequences" activity demonstrating the dangers of alcohol. I use the example of a Halloween party and I choose four audience members to come up on stage. Since it's Halloween, they have to come up with a costume idea and some are pretty hysterical. I give each person an envelope that has the consequence of their drinking for the night. The consequences are: death, DUI, sexual assault and pregnant. Sadly, all of these things may actually happen, and that is what we are trying to prevent. I always hand the "pregnant" envelope to a male because it always gets laughs. Again, we can educate by having fun and I want them to learn that if you're drunk and have unsafe sex, you may end up being a parent. In all the years of doing this activity, yes, I've actually had people who say it has happened to them.

If the program focus is more about drunk driving, I have audience members put on impairment goggles and play catch with a bean bag. First, they toss the bag to make sure they can catch "sober." When they put the goggles on, their hand/eye coordination is impaired. Usually the bean bag sails well above their partner's head. I even use the goggles in my program for DUI offenders, so they can see how impaired they might have been when they drove. Many of them say, "I wouldn't drive feeling like this." But, they did. They did.

For the first twenty minutes of the presentation, I want the audience to know my humor and my personality before I tell them about the crash. Judge Kim Hoover of the Stow Municipal Court in Ohio once told a room of DUI offenders, "Michael is just a big goofy guy who likes KISS. If anyone should be angry, it's him."

The next phase of the program after "playing" with them is the details of the car crash which you've already read. Whether it's a high school student or DUI offender, they lean in closer to hear every word. The room gets quiet, not like "You can hear a pin drop quiet," but even quieter than that. It's an amazing feeling and yet terrifying as I share the intimacy of the crash that changed my life so dramatically. I show the only picture I have of my mom, and me, with Jeff. The picture was taken on one of the days the video was filmed that I described earlier in this book. I have it as an eight-by-ten near my door. On the frame is the necklace she was wearing the night of the crash, her baby bracelet, and an anklet that reads, "Barbara."

I look at that picture every day before I leave. My only mantra in life is to be a son my mother would be proud of. I'm not perfect, but I try my best to be that son she could brag to other friends about.

I have two goals when I leave my apartment. One, to make someone laugh and two, to make a difference in someone's life. If I do that by the time I get back home each evening, then it was a successful day.

I share my story for three main reasons. First, I do it for my mother. Someone has to stand up for her. I cannot let her death be meaningless. Her legacy lives on through me by the program. Her legacy lives on through my brother who teaches kids how to swim. I don't present *The Magic of Life* for sympathy. I don't want people to feel sorry for me, because I've had an amazing life. I do it so others don't have to go through the same pain. I've been coping with the survivors' guilt, depression, and the "what if's" my entire life, I don't want anyone else experiencing it.

The second reason I present my program is for other families who do not have the ability to share their own story. I have met *many* people throughout my life who have been impacted by drunk driving. The National Highway Traffic Safety Administration says that 2 in 3 people will be impacted by drunk driving at some point in their lifetime. I know so many people from social media who have lost their children, husbands, or wives. It's extremely heartbreaking to hear their stories. I once met five strangers in a week and all of them were impacted by drunk driving. When I share my program, I am representing those families. I don't take that responsibility lightly. We want the doors to this "club" closed. Forever...

A few years ago, I was introduced to Christine Moncheck whose son, Andrew, was killed by a drunk driver shortly after graduating from high school. When I met her at a Starbucks, and I heard her emotional story. I thought, "I want her to share her story!" Now, at that time, there is no way she could have done it, she was not ready.

It took a year of gentle coaxing, but Christine has shared her story numerous times in front of DUI offenders. When I hear her speak, I feel that I am lucky not having any memories of my mother. I cannot imagine Christine's pain of losing from her son. I am extremely grateful for her courage and ability to stand up and let others know about Andrew.

Since Christine started speaking with me over the course of the last two years, we have discovered people in our Stow Municipal Court program knew her son. Whether it's a parent or a former classmate of his, they come up and talk with her afterwards, which is quite moving. I watch them offer sympathy and sometimes a hug of comfort. They knew Andrew was killed by a drunk driver and yet, they still chose to drive drunk. It boggles our mind that with that information, they still drove drunk. But then again, Big John knew my story too.

The third reason I do my program is, so you don't have to. This is my life. I don't want this to be yours. I do not want you, your loved ones, or anyone else in my audience to know the effect of impaired driving. Nor do I want you or anyone in the audience to drive impaired and kill someone. If you're a parent and you kill someone, who will look after your kid(s)? I have met DUI offenders who have multiple kids. If you are paying for a DUI, that could be $10,000 not going to your family. Sure, some lawyer is happy, but think of how that affects your family. Recently I had a parent in a program who had ten kids and his DUI was indeed $10,000. I asked him, "What if you were killed, who would look after your kids? How would that impact them?" If that is not incentive enough NOT to drink and drive, I don't know what is.

The Magic of Life program stresses the prevention of driving impaired. Did you know that in the last several years, over 10,000 people have died in this country due to impaired driving. (Yes, I know, another stat!) We have massive debates about gun control and demand for change regarding that, but very little is ever done about drunk driving. How many more people have to die in this country before society stops driving impaired? How many more repeat offenders are allowed back on the roads? No one is saying you cannot drink, but if you're going out, have a plan.

I'd much rather have people use a designated driver within their group than to rely on an Uber or Lyft. Nothing against those companies and their drivers, but I just believe that by having your own DD, it's a better system. We have already seen reports of people being attacked or robbed by a ride-share driver because they were intoxicated. Besides, we teach our kids not to get into cars with strangers but hey, as an intoxicated adult, go ahead and do it. That doesn't make any sense to me. Don't put yourself in a situation where harm can come to you. Besides the fact, as the designated driver, you can drop your drunk friends off at the wrong house and watch them try to get in! Okay...don't...DON'T do that...but if you do, record it for their court hearing. Send me a copy too!

Be the designated driver and tell the bartender or server that you're the designated driver. Maybe you will get free non-alcoholic beverages or a discount on food because you are potentially saving lives that night. Be the hero for the night for your friends. Being the designated driver doesn't mean you have six beers and everyone else has twelve, it means you have ZERO. Take turns among your friends and family too. Because these are the people that care about you and if anything bad did happen to you, they are the ones who will be there, not an Uber driver.

Mothers Against Drunk Driving classifies me as a "victim/survivor" which I vehemently disagree with. Don't you dare call me a victim! I am a survivor! I could have crawled into a bottle and given up, but I didn't. I thank my role models, especially my Dad and Dolly for that. I believe that my mother did not sacrifice her life for me to not live a great life. Survivors overcome adversity and challenges that come their way.

Do I have setbacks with depression? Sure, I do. But I fight hard to survive it. I especially tell DUI offenders, "You have a choice. You can sit there and be a victim of what brought you here tonight, or you can be a survivor of it.

Remember Og Mandino's "The Choice" from an earlier chapter? We all have choices to make in life and we must accept all the responsibility of them of their consequences. I chose to be a survivor, and if you are going through something horrible, you too can be a survivor. But it's entirely up to you.

The word "mom" is not in my vocabulary. Think about that. The word "mom" is not in my vocabulary. It's too precious to me and something that doesn't roll off my tongue very easily. The word "mother" is in my vocabulary though and it's usually followed by another word when I'm stuck in traffic, or in a long line that just isn't moving. You know that word too, right? I was lucky, Dolly has fulfilled every ounce of a mother's role for me, but I have never called her "mom." Jeff and I know she is our mother, and we are her sons. I think calling her Dolly suits her best and I think she would agree. Then again, she didn't want me using her name in this book, so who knows…

Earlier I purposely introduced you to Bryan, Brent, Dennis, Sean and Big John because they are important people in my life. They also fit within the confines of the program. When Big John died, our whole world caved in. If his story can save a life, then showing my pain as I talk about him is worth it. No one wants to experience that type of loss and sharing his story can prevent it from happening to others. A drunk driver told me after a program, "I don't want to end up like Big John.

I wouldn't want to put my family and friends through that."

When I am on a military base and they tell me about all the recent DUI arrests, John's story resonates with them just like it does with the DUI offenders.

I explain to those in the audience that if you continue driving drunk, then you could end up like Big John. I don't want that for you. I don't want *your* family making those phone calls that I had to make.

Everything the military does is built around safety. When I spoke at Barksdale Air Force Base, they were concerned not only due to the amount of DUIs, but the fact some people showed up to their jobs impaired. I helped pack a B-52 bomber parachute, I couldn't imagine doing that impaired.

In one program for MADD near Big John's hometown, an offender told me that he went to high school with him. The impact of hearing about John had a profound effect on him. Hopefully, a long-term effect. I promised The Bev that I would continue sharing her son with the world and his story is paramount for those who think, "Oh, I've driven drunk several times and nothing bad has happened to me."

John thought the same thing and now I visit him in a cemetery. Still to this day, I cry, I laugh, and I yell at him. Just as I stand up for my mother, I stand up for John and his family. I cannot let his death be meaningless either. After all, I made a promise to his mom.

Throughout the program I want people, just like I want you, to think about your purpose in life. I was kept alive for a reason. I try to save lives. Your purpose is not to become a statistic in a police department's ledger of drunk driving arrests or worse, die in a drunk driving crash. Your purpose is to live an amazing life in whatever role you fulfill. You have dreams and goals and a drunk driving arrest can hinder that. During my time at Kent State University, I've seen a student get a DUI and then no longer allowed to become a pilot - dream over! Members of our great military can get discharged or knocked down in rank due to drunk driving. It's time for impaired driving to stop in our country. How many more have to get injured or die when it is so preventable?

I present a lot of programs around prom time and I tell the students, "Your parents do not send you off to prom to die in a drunk driving crash. You are to come back safe and sound so in twenty years you can smile at your prom pictures. Ladies, you will laugh at them and say, "Wow look at my hair!" Guys you will exclaim, "Crap! I used to have hair!!" Realize how precious your lives are before something bad happens.

With college students I explain to them, "Your parents do not send you off to die in college due to alcohol. They send you here to grow as a person, get educated, graduate and get a job." When over 1,500 college students die per year due to alcohol, well, ladies and gentlemen, we have a problem.

As I start to close the program, I share a picture of my footprint on the beach. When I took the picture, I was just playing around with my camera. But when I got home, I saw it in a different light. It made me think that we all have one chance to make that special footprint in life. How many of you have made a footprint in the sand by the ocean? What happens moments later? A wave comes and washes it away. Think of that footprint as your life. We have this one chance to leave behind our legacy, our footprint.

As I mention to my DUI audience, "You've made one footprint getting into the courtroom with your DUI. When you leave this room, you have a chance to start anew. You have a chance to create a brand-new footprint when you step outside. How will you live your life now?" I continue, "The footprint that brought you in here has washed away, you can make a fresh one."

As a comedian, I learned that you need a strong closing bit to end your set and I looked to my musical idols for inspiration for my closer. KISS closes each show with *Rock and Roll All Night* and cannons shoot tons of white confetti into the crowd as fireworks go off. There is so much confetti that it looks like it's snowing. I've been front row before, and you can hardly see the stage. You feel the heat of the fireworks and hear the audience singing along with the band. Now, *that* leaves a long-lasting impression and a smile on everyone's face. The "water trick" was a great closing bit for many years, but I needed something better, more profound and meaningful that fits what *The Magic of Life* has become. I needed a

Rock and Roll All Night to close the program. Just without the fireworks and confetti.

When I stopped closing with the disappearing water trick years ago, I stumbled upon my new closer one day from swimming, of all things. I was swimming sets and brought my fingers up to my neck to feel my pulse to check my heart rate. As if a light bulb went off above my head, I thought how great it was to feel my pulse and be alive even though at the time I was huffing and puffing on the wall. I just focused on my heartbeat. It was like a drum beat against my fingers as I considered my next set. It inspired me to close the program by having the audience close their eyes and focus on their heartbeat. What I would like for you to do right now is take your forefinger and middle finger and hold them against your neck. Feel your pulse. Close your eyes and just focus on your heartbeat for about twenty seconds.

You know what that means when you can feel that, don'tcha? That's right, YOU'RE ALIVE! So, whenever you're having a bad day, close your eyes for a few seconds, feel your pulse and realize how awesome it is to be alive.

My largest audience of 4,000 freshmen at Kent State University

Living my purpose presenting *The Magic of Life* at

Brecksville/Broadview Hts Middle School

Chapter 27

The Impact of The Magic of Life

When I started *The Magic of Life*, I never knew the impact it would have not only on those in the audience, but also on me. I am extremely honored to share my program, just like I am grateful that you are holding this book in your hands. I relive the emotional pain every time I speak but it's worth it to save a life. I may never know the long- term effect this program has on people, but if it inspires just one person, just one, to never drive impaired again, or ever, then I have served my purpose.

There are times when I open the floor to questions, and I get some of the best questions about the crash from DUI offenders. It makes me realize that I do make a difference. In the beginning, I never thought I would speak in front of DUI offenders. If I can prevent one person from driving impaired after the program, then it's a fabulous day at "the office."

Throughout my life, I've carried a lot of anger towards drunk drivers, especially Harvey. Fortunately, I don't carry that anger with me into the DUI programs. "My anger is reserved for one person, Harvey who killed my mother. If I took out my anger on you then it would be misplaced. You didn't do anything to me. If I stay angry my entire life, Harvey wins, and I am too competitive for that to happen. He already took my mother, he will not take my soul," I explain to the offenders each time. Presenting for the Stow Court as part of Judge Hoover's intervention program and for MADD, has been some of the most rewarding work I've ever done as a speaker. After the first program I did at the court, a young woman who was just nineteen said, "Thank you for making me realize my son needs me more than I need alcohol."

During a Q&A at Minot Air Force Base, an Airman asked me, "If you could say one thing to the man that killed your mother, what would it be?" Tough question and some audience members bristled at it. I am not sure why I got so emotional at that moment, but I had to pause, look at the floor and compose myself. I could feel the pressure of the tears in the corners of my eyes. That uncomfortable lump in my throat returned as I struggled to get my words out. They weren't words of hatred for the drunk driver, but when I could finally open my mouth, I said, "That he robbed me of my mother."

At the end of the program, we hand out *The Magic of Life* wristbands that have the following printed on it:

The Magic of Life   I pledge not to drink and drive BG AM JK

When the DUI offenders choose to take one after the program, it makes me feel validated because they made the decision to change their lives. They made that pledge for themselves, for their families, and for all the innocent people out on the roads. They take one to honor Barbara Gershe, Andrew Moncheck and John Kelly. I'm especially thrilled when the probation officers at the Stow Municipal Court tell me that offenders were still wearing *The Magic of Life* wristband months after the program. Either the program really made a difference, or the wristband is just an awesome fashion statement. Gene Simmons was happy to wear one too when I met him.

When I present *The Magic of Life*, I do not hold back, even if things get a little dark. I've opened up about my depression on stage because I want people to know that they are not alone. I remember talking to one young college student for about an hour after a program regarding her depression. She said, "If you didn't talk about it tonight, I may have done something this week."

She felt safe sharing her struggles with me after hearing me talk about mine. I will never forget it. If you are suffering from depression, you are not alone. You can always get help.

It is never easy to share your feelings onstage, but someone is always out there who needs to hear the message. We are just starting to have a better dialogue about depression and suicide in this country. Unfortunately, we are a long way away from making it comfortable for people to talk about it freely. I know I've struggled talking about it with others, but, when I have talked about it, I feel so much better.

Another incredible outcome of the program is the ability to inspire others who have been impacted by drunk driving to share their stories. Your story needs to be heard. I've seen Christine Moncheck speak for almost two years now. On one occasion she received a standing ovation from police officers. That was so powerful, it nearly made me cry. Like so many other parents, she is trying to make sure others don't bury their kids. Is it easy? Hell no, but her story affects so many people.

I met an Airman at Minot Air Force Base that was in a horrific drunk driving crash where the drunk driver died. When I met her, she was on crutches. She spent a long time in a wheelchair recovering from her massive injuries. After hearing her lengthy list of broken bones, in a way, it made me glad I was an infant when I suffered from my own. She said I inspired her to share her story. She has gone on to tell her story and make a difference in people's lives. Knowing you are not alone in a cause is a wonderful feeling and if I can help someone share their story, then I am incredibly happy and blessed.

The Magic of Life eventually led me to develop a diversity program called *Jewish Born, Jamaican Raised* (JBJR). *The Magic of Life* honors my mother and JBJR pays homage to Dolly. During this program we discuss racism, anti-Semitism, and healthy ways to cope. My father and Dolly taught me values which helped me through life. With this program, it's just not me sharing my story, but also how others have coped with discrimination. We can all learn from each other. Since hate is a learned behavior, people can learn NOT to hate.

Back to *The Magic of Life*. After one program at a middle school on the west side of Chicago a student asked me, "If you could go back and change where the car crash didn't happen, would you?"

Whoa, that's a deep question. Such a tough one to answer, because obviously I would love it if my mom was alive, but at the same time, I have had a good life and the opportunity to impact so many lives. If it wasn't for the crash, I wouldn't have Dolly in my life and its hard imagining life without her. Would life be different? Sure would. Yet, this is the only life I've known, and I made the best of it.

Would I have gone on to be a comedian if the crash didn't happen? Or would I have been a doctor? Would I go back and change it? I honestly don't know, but because of the difference I have made with *The Magic of Life*, my answer has me leaning towards...

The Magic of Life has also given me the opportunity to branch out in the community as well. In

April 2015, along with Andy Shockney and Chief Jack Davis of the Cuyahoga Falls Police Department, we formed The Magic of Life Foundation, a non-profit organization. Our mission is to help prevent impaired driving by presenting the program to any community that wants it. So many schools tell us, "We want the program, but we lack funding." I simply cannot go to California when a school has just $200 in their budget. I thought if we had a non-profit organization, then we can get local businesses to help sponsor the program. Preventing impaired driving is a community responsibility, so why not get them involved?

Getting them involved is the toughest part. We'd love to have a corporate sponsorship that would help us get our message out. It is a win-win situation. The company gets to promote their business and show they are a partner in making communities safer.

We also want to help children impacted by drunk driving. Jeff and I had Dolly for help, what other kid is going to have that type of luck?

Another goal is to provide student scholarships in honor of my mother, Barbara, and Andrew Moncheck. I may be over my head in figuring out how to run a non-profit organization, but we will eventually succeed. We are pretty dedicated to the mission and goals. We have been fortunate to have amazing people help us make our vision reality. Could we use more help? Absolutely.

I think it would be incredible to have a roster of speakers across the country to be a part of our foundation who believe in our "learn, laugh, inspire" theme. There are many people who have powerful, inspirational stories that need to be told.

The impact our organization made in the community was felt on June 8th, 2018 when we held our first fundraiser. It included a buffet, comedy show, silent auction, and Top Cop DUI awards. I had three amazing friends, Greg Smrdel, Mike Conley and Jeff Blanchard who are great supporters of the program, and some of the funniest people I know, perform that night. We awarded nine local officers for their DUI enforcement. It was an honor. We raised some money, had a lot of laughs, and gave special recognition to the officers out there making our streets safer on a daily basis.

The foundation also presented Judge Kim Hoover of the Stow Municipal Court a special award for his intervention program, which has no doubt changed so many people's lives in the community. We are glad to be able to present our program each month as part of his initiative. Oh, and how's this for fate? If it wasn't for comedy, I never would have met the Judge. His bailiff is a former waitress at the comedy club where I first started.

The Magic of Life has also made my dad and Dolly proud of the man I have become. Many years ago, I presented the program at a Temple in Boca Raton for students and their parents. I was excited and nervous all at the same time because I had family members and lifelong friends attend. The program has changed so much since the first time my dad and Dolly saw it. I wanted it perfect that night. Spinal Stenosis and Parkinson's disease started to affect my father's mobility, but nothing was going to stop him from seeing his son that night.

Although I couldn't see my father's reaction during the program, when I saw him afterward, he was beaming just like he did during my Bar Mitzvah. While I didn't have his notes of "SLOW DOWN," I remembered his words of wisdom. He took my hand when we had a moment to ourselves and said, "I'm very proud of you Michael. Your mother would be proud of you. You're doing a wonderful thing with this program."

On May 25, 2016, I was in the middle of a program at Minot Air Force Base. I stood under a huge American flag in the hospital's atrium where over a hundred Airmen listened attentively. I stopped to call my father for his birthday. I put him on speaker phone, and said, "Happy Birthday Dad," then had the Airmen sing Happy Birthday to him. He said, "Thank you very much, I'm proud of you and I love you." I got very emotional and turned my back to the audience until I composed myself to finish the program.

My father would often say, "I'm proud of you" often and even wrote it on my birthday cards for the last couple of years. When I would visit him at his assisted living facility in South Florida, his friends would say, "Oh, you're Michael, I've heard so much about you." The staff would tell me, "Your father is a very funny man, you must get your humor from him." My dad would correct them and say, "No, I get my humor from him," pointing at me. What else could a son want other than to hear his father was proud of him?

After my program in Boca with my Dad and brother.

Chapter 28

"You're a 48-year-old orphan"

On January 25th, 2018, my father Martin, passed away after an eight-year battle with Parkinson's disease. Following forty-seven years of an insurmountable weight of grief on his shoulders, he rejoined his beloved wife Barbara.

When I look back at my father and what he had to cope with, not only with the grief of my mother, but also his own fight with Parkinson's, I realize my father was one of the strongest people I have ever known. I never heard him say, "Why did this happen to me?" While I may have said because of all his hospital visits and health struggles, "How much more can he take?" I don't ever recall hearing him say that. And he had a lot of hospital visits.

In the weeks prior to his passing, his oxygen levels would drop, and we thought he would need an oxygen tank to help him breath. As I flew down on January 23rd, I had no idea how bad he was until I got to the hospital. Jeff kept on saying, "It's not good, it's not good" on the drive from the airport. I figured my dad would rebound like he often did.

He was intubated over the weekend and was still in the ICU. With his oxygen levels low, the doctors put him on a BiPap machine, a non-invasive ventilator to help him breathe normally. He wore a mask that looked like a scuba diving mask over his face.

Dad had a collapsed lung along with pneumonia. Not a good combination. With the mask on and him feeling so weak, he couldn't talk to us. His mind was strong, but his body was failing him. I was grateful that the room next to him was vacant as I would occasionally go in there, pray and cry after seeing my father in this condition. My brother and I knew about his decision of what to do in this situation. We wanted to obey his wishes; however, we also didn't want to face the reality of signing off on them.

The next day, he was still alert. The doctors wanted to see if he could breathe without the BiPap machine, so they tried a regular oxygen mask. Once the nurse put the mask over his nose, he would repeat in a raspy whisper, "Take it off, take it off, take it off."

I knew he meant he didn't want to go on anymore, but I pretended he was talking about the blanket draped across him. When I looked into my father's eyes, I could tell he was tired of the fight. You can tell a lot from what a person is thinking with their eyes when they cannot talk. Shortly after they put him on the regular oxygen mask, he could not sustain a high enough level, so they put him back on the BiPap machine. He would look up at us with his big brown eyes and you could tell he was scared.

Communicating with us was difficult until the nurse gave him a laminated paper that had a keyboard on it. He would point to letters and I would write them out. Not even sure how he could see the letters properly through the mask without his glasses, but he did. With Jeff, Dolly and me by his side, we were able to talk with him as he continued to point to letters. Moving his hand slowly he would spell out, "You can change the channel. No game show." He even told us, "Tell Dolly not to come back without noodle pudding." Even in this condition, he still had his sense of humor and appetite for Dolly's great cooking. I felt like I was on "Wheel of Fortune" guessing his phrases. One time I couldn't figure out what he was spelling, and he spelled out, "Are you dum?" which made us laugh.

Dolly really didn't want to leave his side, but I took her over to her sister's house. Dolly's sister was battling her own fight with cancer. She told my dad, "Marty you hang in there and we'll see you later. I love you."

Dolly has always been so strong for everyone else, but it was my turn to be her anchor through this difficult time. If I could get her to laugh, then it helped reduce a little of the stress for her. Her worry and concern was insurmountable.

My father asked for some of his pictures that he took when he was much younger. As I mentioned earlier, he was great photographer. I sat in that room with him, I wondered why he never shared more of his pictures with us. I often wondered why he never pursued it as a career, but I never asked. He had some "mad skills" with the camera when they used film. This was all before our current high-tech digital cameras.

On my laptop, I decided to show him pictures I took and was proud of. As I scrolled through them all, he made me stop and pointed to one that I had taken on a trail. The picture was a little American Flag on a fence post by a local cemetery. As he pointed at it, he looked at me as to say, "Did you take that? That's really good."

I smiled. We went through several pictures and then looked at a few articles he did for Dolly's tennis leagues. He was proud of his work and rightly so. He may have been an accountant by trade, but behind the lens, he was a gifted photographer.

Throughout my life, my father showed enthusiasm in everything I did, but now the roles were reversed as we looked at his pictures. I was cherishing the time I had left with him. It was a great bonding moment as we shared our passions. I regret not getting into photography earlier in my life. Weeks earlier I mailed him a 2018 *Magic of Life* calendar. The calendar was 12 of my favorite pictures I had taken in Northeast Ohio, Italy and Virginia.

I was unsure if he ever saw it between all of his recent hospital stays. The staff at his assisted living facility said it was not among his mail. As we continued to look at our photographs, I told him, "See Dad? Your love for photography finally rubbed off on me." It was priceless. The sand in the hourglass was running out but I wanted, no, I needed, more time with him.

Later that day he asked me if he had to be intubated again. He did not want to be. He spelled out, "Am I going to die?" "No, you will recover like you have always done in the past," I told him as I tried to be as positive as possible. His thoughts were lucid, and he asked if his sister, Susan, who was currently fighting cancer knew about his condition. We were keeping our family informed and they offered their support. The doctors kept giving us updates on his lungs. They were not pushy but wanted us to sign the form about concerning my father's wishes because he was not going to get any better.

When we asked him, "Do you want to be intubated again?" He shook his head no several times. Jeff and I joked that even though it was his wishes we could just disobey him like when we were kids. We did not want him to suffer anymore, but at the same time didn't want to sign those papers. But we did. As Jeff reluctantly signed the paper, the reality of losing my Dad washed over me. I entered that vacant room next to his, my own little sanctuary, and started to tremble as tears ran down my face. After a few moments I composed myself and returned to my father's room. I wanted to be strong for him.

My father asked for his friend Victor, who was big into prayer to stop by, but unfortunately, Victor could not make it. Instead we put Victor on speaker phone. Jeff sat on one side of the bed, and I on the other as we held our father's hands. My Dad stroked my hand with his thumb to comfort me as Victor said a beautiful prayer.

He also requested the Rabbi from his assisted living facility by spelling it out on the keyboard. Somehow, he just knew his time was coming. Like I said earlier, his eyes said he was ready to rejoin my mother. As we waited for the Rabbi, he spelled out, "I love you." In which I responded with my tears in my eyes, "I love you too Dad."

The machine continued to do all his breathing for him. The Rabbi arrived and led us through another prayer as my father once again stroked my hand with his thumb. Even though I understood what was happening, it was still like an out of body experience. I have never been a very observant Jew and throughout my life had my arguments with God. However, at that moment, I prayed that my father would not suffer anymore. Despite this plea, I also didn't want him to go.

When you know time is limited with someone, you tend to stress out a bit and wonder, "How much time do I have to tell them so much?" I have so much more I need to say.

Soon after the Rabbi left, Dad fell asleep again as Jeff and I sat in the room each deep in our own thoughts. The noises from the various machines permeated the air. Before I left for the night, leaving Jeff there for a little bit longer, I said, "Goodnight Dad, see you tomorrow, I love you." Not sure if he heard me, but at least I said it one last time.

Jeff knocked on my door around 6:15 a.m. but I was already up after a restless night. He simply said, "The hospital called, he passed."

After a long sigh and more tears, I got up and hugged my brother. We knew this was going to happen, but it didn't make it any easier. As we were about to turn down the road leading to the hospital, Dolly's son-in-law, Audley, called for a status update. I told him, "He passed away a bit earlier this morning. We will come over soon and tell Dolly." Telling her was going to be so daunting, I certainly did not want to do it. After all, I was the youngest sibling, that's the responsibility of the oldest!

With the amount of times my dad was in the hospital, every nurse, aide and doctor had been incredibly wonderful. The nurse that greeted us as we made our way to his room was no exception. His words comforted us as he said, "It was nice to see family here. We don't always see that. It really made a difference with your father." He was so compassionate when he said, "Take your time with him," as we were about to enter Dad's room.

The room was eerily quiet without the hum and buzz of the machines. I looked upon my father. Having those precious moments with him were so important as I started to reflect on what he meant to me. It was difficult seeing him but yet comforting knowing he was not struggling after such a long battle. Jeff and I left his room after a few minutes to find the nurse. We said, "We have one more family member who needs to see him." With that we were off to tell Dolly and bring her back to see him.

As Jeff and I walked up to the front door of her home, we both looked at each other and said, "Well, who is going to tell her?" I must have lost a bet somewhere in life because the responsibility fell on me. So much for being the youngest sibling and getting out of this job.

Dolly was lying in bed with some game show on. I sat down on the bed, put my hand on her shoulder as she asked, "How is he today?"

All of a sudden, I felt like the parent as I paused and slowly said, "Dolly, he passed away this morning."

"NO! NO!" she shouted as she did a one-hundred-eighty-degree flip on the bed.

I reached down to hug her. Shit, I thought telling my friends about Big John was tough, but this was a whole other level of pain. Jeff entered her room to hug her too as we cried together.

The three of us headed back to the hospital so she could have her time with him, and we could start making whatever arrangements we had to make. I am not even sure we said anything in the car or in the elevator up to his floor. Jeff and I walked slowly on each side of Dolly for support. We pulled the curtain back a little bit and entered his room as a family. A family that was brought together by fate. Jeff and I then stepped out, so she could have her alone time with a man that, over time, she fell in love with and vice versa. Forty-seven years together, with ups and downs like in any relationship, but with definitely more ups than downs. She was so heartbroken but said, "At least you're not suffering anymore Marty and you're back with your beloved Barbara."

Jeff and I met with the funeral director to begin the memorial and funeral arrangements. Jeff has the best swim school in Broward County, Florida called Just Swim. During the summer he gives lessons at a local Temple and asked the Rabbi to lead our father's memorial service. The Rabbi wanted to know more about our dad and gave us words of comfort. In his large office surrounded by massive bookcases he said, "You guys are now, technically, orphans." Anyone want to adopt a 48-year-old man/child? I'm housebroken...Just sayin'.

I told the Rabbi that I would give a eulogy and Jeff said he would write his up and give it to the Rabbi to say. Despite spending the last 20 plus years in public speaking, the Rabbi reminded me how giving a eulogy is the toughest thing to do. Thanks Rabbi, no pressure.

The funeral director said we could also show a photo montage of Dad before the service. Jeff, along with his girlfriend, and I poured over hundreds of photographs. We selected about thirty of them to use. There were so many incredible pictures of Dad throughout his life. Some of the pictures were from when he was a baby. Some as a teenager. Others showed him a bit older from his time in the service. I sat there slowly looking at all the pictures wondering why he never shared them with us. It was the pictures with my mother that I felt the saddest about.

Why didn't he share these? It felt like I was discovering a man I didn't know. Jeff and I explored our father's life in those photographs. We wanted to make sure the montage captured the spirit of him perfectly. When people saw the pictures, we wanted them to smile and say, "Yup, that was Marty."

Unfortunately, my Aunt Susan, who was weak from her cancer could not make the memorial service. I wrote several drafts of my father's eulogy and sent her some copies to get her opinion. I must have written over thirty variations of what I was going to say. I was grateful that the service was live online so my aunt and other family members who could not attend would be able to watch.

The woman with whom I had been dating for a few months flew down from her home in Detroit for the service. I was extremely grateful that she had, although, I am not sure if a memorial service is the best time to meet someone's family. But she really helped me get through it.

The morning of my father's service, I took her down to the Fort Lauderdale beach across from the Swimming Hall of Fame, where I spent much of my youth, for some much needed "beach therapy." With my camera, I embraced my father's love of photography. I took several pictures, including the one of my footprints that I now use in my program. As we stood on the beach, my mind was focused on giving the eulogy in a couple of hours.

I saw cousins that I hadn't seen in years and jokingly re-introduced myself to them, which when you think about it, a memorial service is a bad time to do that. But hey, humor helps in situations like this, right?

When it was time for the last viewing, I gathered my strength and approached my father who looked so peaceful. I know I keep coming back to that word, but he really did. I placed my only KISS tie, a *The Magic of Life* wristband and calendar into the casket with him. I silently said a prayer for him and started to think about my eulogy once again. Being a comedian for all these years makes one paranoid and we tend to look at our "set" numerous times. I just had to remember my dad's advice - *slow down*.

As we sat in the first row, I held Dolly's hand. The Rabbi started the service as the video montage continued to play. He read a letter from a cousin who shared many great memories of my father. My cousin Steven spoke next also reliving many memories of my dad. The two of them were extremely close. He mentioned the car crash which made me tremble and Dolly put her arm around me for comfort.

When it was my turn to speak, I tried to practice some deep breathing that I remembered from my attempts at yoga to help calm me down. I took my eulogy out of my jacket pocket looked out at my family and friends and said to myself, "Here we go, the Rabbi was right, this is going to be tough." I figured I would start out with one of my favorite jokes I wrote about my father to try and get people to laugh, but also to calm my nerves.

A tie for Father's Day!

After Jeff's
Bar Mitzvah, 1980

At Jeff's 50th surprise party June 24, 2017.

Looking at my Dad's pictures with him in the hospital
January 24, 2018, the day before he passed.

Chapter 29

Remembering Dad

I stood at the podium. My palms were sweaty, and I thought my heart would leap out of my chest. I stared at the paper and reminded myself to "slow down" as I began my father's eulogy:

When I was younger, my dad wanted me to learn on my own and when I couldn't spell a word, I would ask him, "Hey Dad, how do you spell this word? He would say, go look it up in the dictionary. I can't, I don't know HOW to spell it! He would tell me, "Well, sound it out." Yeah, great advice to give your kid who is in speech therapy. 'Tanks Dad, I wuve you.too!'

It should not be a sad day for us as we remember my dad. After 47 years he is finally back with his wife and our mother. He is finally at peace after battling all his health issues, not letting Parkinson's hold him back. I cannot imagine the internal pain he went through after the car crash that he carried around 47 years. He carried that with him and that made him one of the strongest men I ever knew.

I just want to share with you some of my favorite memories and how he impacted my life which gives you an idea of the man my father was. No matter what we did, his passion was just the same as ours, if not more. For swimming, he would drive us to morning practice and sleep in the car as we swam. He became an official, even disqualifying me and a lot of my friends. His passion for the sport was sometimes greater than mine. He taught me how hard work pays off and to stay focused on my goals.

He was not a KISS fan and only told me to turn the music down, never off. He and Dolly drove me to my very first KISS concert, how cool was that? He did it because he knew how much it meant to me. Or, he just didn't trust me driving the car! He even bought me little paint brushes, so I could dust my KISS Bobbleheads!

Proud is a good word to describe how dad felt about us. Proud because we were his sons, he loved bragging about. I'd like to think he was bragging to our mother as well.

With magic, he would buy me tricks until I could pay for them myself. He loved when I would practice them in front of him and Dolly. He drove me to magic club *meetings and to gigs when I didn't have my license. When the magic case in the store was $200, well out of our price range, we went to Home Depot and bought $60 worth of wood and supplies and built one together. I still have it today.*

When we got into trains as a hobby for what it seemed like a day, dad helped us build a huge train table and showed such enthusiasm for it. He built Jeff a rabbit cage that really seemed like a penthouse for that thing, and he wasn't even a fan of pets. Dad REALLY didn't like Mickey, my cockatiel bird that would run out from underneath his lazy boy chair and attack his feet when he would walk by. He would call him 'dirty bird' which of course Mickey would repeat.

Before I learned how to type, he would stay up late typing my papers. I would often wake up and hear the typewriter's bell in the middle of the night and find my paper waiting for me when I woke up for school. He always wore shirts with a front left pocket that had a cross pen in it.

Dad always drove with both feet which I thought was the correct way to drive until I learned how to actually drive. I remember thinking, what do you mean you only drive with one foot? My dad uses two, he's right and you are wrong.

When dad visited me in Ohio for one of my many surgeries, I had an electrical cord that ran under a rug. That wasn't safe enough for him, so he made me an extension cord and framed it around the door. I'm pretty sure he broke things, just so he could fix them again. He could fix almost anything.

He supported my comedy. Name any other dad who after his son spent two years in graduate school who then said was going to pursue comedy instead of looking for a real job and didn't get mad. He didn't say 'No' or 'Are you crazy??!!" He just said, "Okay, go for it." He knew how much I loved comedy and when my favorite comedians were on Carson, he would let me stay up late to see them. He always wanted to know about my shows and where I was performing next.

My dad loved playing the organ, which he got me into as well. It was cool to share that with him for a while. Even with his Parkinson's, he played, and he loved playing for people. I will always remember him playing and filling our home with music. He even organized a kazoo band at his assisted living facility and wanted to take it out on the road! Should have gotten him on America's Got Talent. Just what America needs, a senior citizen kazoo band!

He loved photography so much that it rubbed off on Jeff while growing up and most recently, me too. I wish I told him more about my love for it, so we could have shared that together. At least I was able to show him some pictures last week that he liked. That brings me some comfort. His favorite late-night snack was bowtie pasta and cottage cheese. I've never had it, but I just may have to see what the old man liked about it.

When I started presenting The Magic of Life in honor of my mother, and to make sure other people didn't go through what he did, he was extremely proud. I am just grateful he had the chance to see it in person. I even stopped a program on his birthday at Minot Air Force Base to call him for his birthday and have the Airmen sing happy birthday to him. He told me how proud he was of me for making sure my mother's legacy lived on.

He showed me how to tie a tie, cut a piece of wood in a straight line and he made the best matzo brei during Passover. Something I cannot even re-create. He just had the magic touch. His only career advice to me was "Do something you enjoy and make lots of money." Well, I went into education, so one out of two isn't bad.

And how can I talk about him without speaking of Dolly, even though she will probably punch me—I will scream child abuse, I got witnesses this time. But out of something so tragic, Dolly came into our lives. The best way I can sum up her impact on us after 47 years is that not only did you save me and Jeff by helping to raise us, but you saved dad. You were his rock through everything. You brought him smiles, laughter and amazing memories.

He let us be us and encouraged us to pursue our own dreams no matter what they were. He was proud to be our father and we are proud to be his sons. I am glad the I had chance to thank him for being my father and tell him that I loved him.

I sat back down, smiled at my brother as I sighed and said, "See, it wasn't *that* hard."

The Rabbi was correct, it was the hardest speech I ever had to give.

The Rabbi then read what Jeff wrote. For someone who says he isn't good in those "right" brain activities, Jeff wrote a beautiful eulogy for our father.

The next day my girlfriend helped me clean out my father's room at the assisted living facility. If it wasn't for her help, I'd probably still be in there. The task would have been too emotional for Jeff and me to do on our own. Jeff spent way more time there than I did so I totally understand how painful it would have been for him. My dad turned into a little hoarder over the years, and I felt myself learning more about him as we went through the room. It seemed that he kept everything! He kept my piano books from when I was in Junior High and his old transistor radio that didn't even work anymore.

One nice thing is that we were able to donate his clothes and some other things to his fellow residents. I donated his record player and most of his CDs to the facility so other people could enjoy the music. The aides came in like scavengers. They wanted his tv, electric piano and other items. They all said, "Oh Marty said I could have that." I didn't have the strength to argue with them and I am sure he would have wanted them to have whatever he promised them.

Our father would be buried next to our mother on Long Island. Jeff, along with his girlfriend and I headed to New York for the burial.

As we checked into the hotel, one of the rooms was 525, our father's birthday. I recognized it right away and exclaimed, "Look at the room number! How's that for a sign?" We just stared at each other and smiled at the coincidence.

Our cousin Randy who lives in New York was our "family tour guide." She took us through Brooklyn, showing us where my dad lived and grew up. It was fun to head down memory lane to my grandparent's apartment. I remember playing in their kitchen with an orange ice cream scooper Nana gave me. For some weird reason, I also remember walking down the hallway to the garbage chute to toss their trash. We also drove past Erasmus High School where my dad roamed the hallways as a teenager along with Barbara Streisand.

It was a sunny, but yet chilly January day for his burial on Long Island. Before the ceremony we placed rocks on everyone's headstone as per the Jewish tradition. The Rabbi who led the service was fantastic and made it a lot easier to get through. There was only a few of us, but he led the service as if there were hundreds in attendance.

As I looked down at his casket, I knew my father and mother were together again.

And just as we did for my grandfather years earlier, we each took a shovel of dirt and placed it onto my father's casket My cousin Randy read my Aunt Susan's statement since she could not be there. In her statement, she wrote, *I plan to do my best to maintain the special relationships I have with each of your boys. So even though I can't be there today, it's time to say goodbye to my brother Martin.*

As we eventually drove away from the cemetery, I knew both my parents would be watching over me.

Chapter 30

Missing Dad, Evading Grief

After my father's burial, I flew back to south Florida to say goodbye to Dolly. Then it was time to head back to Ohio where life was waiting for me. I barely slept. I stopped working out. I just put my head down and went back to work without really taking time to grieve.

My first program after his death was on February 15th at the Stow Municipal Court. I really didn't want to do it either. I didn't feel like telling jokes or talking about the crash.

As I set up in the courtroom, Steve, one of the probation officers, took one look at me and knew something was wrong. It's amazing when people who know you well can tell something is wrong just by looking at you. You may think you're hiding your pain inside, but some people can see right through your facade. Steve gave me some words of encouragement which was something I really needed at that moment.

Once I started the program and I heard some laughter from the DUI offenders, I was in my world where I felt safe. I didn't feel so depressed during the presentation and was able to impact lives that night. Once the program was over, all those difficult emotions came rushing back over me like water over a broken dam. The important thing, however, is that for ninety minutes, I was living my purpose and making my parents proud.

My brother was inducted to LaSalle University's Athletes Hall of Fame on February 17th, which was such a great honor. While he knew Jeff was going to be inducted it was difficult not having the opportunity to share the moment with our dad.

This time Jeff couldn't hand his speech over to anyone to deliver for him. Despite this, he delivered a funny and passionate speech about his time swimming and how much this honor meant to him. He also dedicated it to our father. I was Jeff's "photographer" for the event, and I couldn't help but get choked up during his speech. I was so proud of Jeff. This was our first major family event we couldn't share with our father. Later on, I called Dolly to tell her how everything went. She, of course, was elated.

The day after Jeff's induction, I made my way to see Gene Simmons in Philadelphia with my long-time friend and favorite redhead, Dennis. We almost went deaf standing outside the Trocadero in Chinatown during Chinese New Year. The sheer volume of firecrackers that went off while we waited for two hours outside made my ears ring the rest of the day.

But even as we waited for Gene, I didn't feel like myself. In previous times where I met the band, I felt like a kid. But with the recent loss of my father, I just felt off. I told Gene about my father and that I placed my KISS tie in his casket. He gave me some heartfelt words.

I told him about *The Magic of Life* at a previous event in 2016, but I decided to tell him again. When I showed him *The Magic of Life* wristband, he smiled and held out his arm for me to put it on him. We took several pictures of him displaying the wristband. Say what you want about Gene, but he genuinely cares about his fans.

I asked Gene if he would record a short message that I could play during the program and he said, "Okay, no problem." With Dennis grinning from ear to ear behind the camera, Gene gave me a 26 second statement in which he called me "Gershe" which was awesome! Gene also signed a picture of him breathing fire, that I took at Detroit's Cobo Hall in 2009 before it closed down.

Gene held it up to show the man who was helping with the event and said with a huge smile, "This is incredible!"

In those few minutes with Gene, I experienced something that I hadn't felt in a while—happiness. I wished I could have called my father to tell him about the experience.

The weekend after my brother's induction and my meeting with Gene Simmons, I gave my first TEDxTalk at Kent State University. I had been working on it for months trying to fit a 60-minute program into thirteen minutes. Since I had a tendency to rush, I remembered my dad's advice to "*slow down.*" In attendance was my girlfriend, a fellow co-worker, and a board member who was also a classmate of mine in graduate school. I was grateful for their support as I was really a nervous wreck. I had edited this presentation so many times, and I wanted it perfect. I put so much pressure on myself that I had to also remind myself to relax and have fun with it.

As I stood backstage waiting my turn, I stretched, did some deep breathing and prayed that I had the strength not to screw it up. I had a wireless headset microphone which made me feel like I was in a boy band. I also had used a clicker for the presentation and one thing that pissed me off was that they said it wasn't working right. Most of all the other speakers were also presenting for the first time and you're going to give us a problematic clicker? I wanted to yell, "Bullshit, get one that works!" But I didn't want to cause a scene, my nerves were already frazzled.

When my opening joke landed solidly with laughs (too bad you can't hear them on the Ted Talk video) I felt like I was in my zone. Sure enough, the clicker didn't work right and internally I wanted to scream so loud, but I didn't let it bother me on stage. I had to honor my father by keeping calm and do what I do best. In an audience of over 200 people, a few came up to say they too have been impacted by drunk driving. I was happy with the presentation, but the one person I wanted to call was now looking down upon me. I could feel something was wrong with me. I was finally starting to grieve. Or so I thought.

I found myself coping by eating poorly, which was great for my taste buds, but bad for my waistline. I struggled to get out of bed, but I continued showing up for work, and while I was physically there, mentally I was somewhere else. I was advising an average of ten students each day. If I took a sick day, they wouldn't be advised, and it would just be more stress for me. I just pushed through it and my moods changed as quickly as the Ohio weather. Instead of dealing with my grief, I focused on the program and *The Magic of Life* fundraiser that was coming up in June. I slacked off going to the gym and stopped writing daily jokes on Facebook. The only time I felt like myself was when I presented my program. I was miserable the rest of the time and just avoided grieving. If life couldn't get any worse, well, it was about to.

In the months after my father's passing, my aunt's health continued to decline. She was in a lot of pain from Lymphedema. We talked often. She would keep me up to date on how she was doing. What she was really doing was preparing me for her pending death.

In late April, Aunt Sue told me she was in her house but getting hospice care. We choked back tears as we said "I love you" many times. I didn't want to believe that she could die so soon and tried to remain positive. We just lost my father and now, now God was about to put us through another death? No, I wouldn't accept this. But it was a sad, harsh reality.

Jeff and I at his LaSalle University's
Athletes Hall of Fame induction, 2/17/18

Dennis and I with Gene Simmons on 2/18/18

TedxTalk at
Kent State on
2/24/18

Chapter 31

Aunt Sue

On Monday, April 23rd, I presented a program at high school in Connecticut, and since I was so close to the cemetery, went for a quick visit before my flight. It was another sunny day on Long Island, and I had a few conversations with my loved ones. The family plot was filling up with people I really missed. I just wanted to sit down and stay there all day, but I had a plane to catch. I said my goodbyes and promised I would be back when I could.

I called my Aunt Sue on Wednesday, April 25th and she sounded like a totally different person than she did just a few days ago. She was moved to the hospice care facility and her voice sounded weak. I didn't want to keep her on the phone too long. I knew they were making her as comfortable as possible with medication. I told her I loved her. "Why can't I have the Barbara Bush treatment?" she asked referring to Mrs. Bush who passed away after stopping her treatment. My aunt didn't want to suffer anymore.

On April 27th, I pulled into the fire station parking lot in Poland, Ohio two hours before my program at Poland Seminary High School. The fire station was sponsoring the program and invited me for lunch. My Uncle Michael had just texted me: "The doctors said that Susan only has a couple of days left."

I called him to get more information and to see how he was doing. If I could have left for the airport right then and there, I would have. Unfortunately, I had a program to do and not only that, I was filming it for a new promotional video.

Instead of focusing on the program, I was now mentally and emotionally destroyed. My world was crushed and to think I was just at the cemetery four days ago. I couldn't believe I was going to have to back so soon for another family burial.

During the five-minute drive from the fire station to the school, tears streamed down my face as I thought about my aunt.

As I waited for the program to start backstage, I likely paced a mile. I was focused on my aunt, but I had to put all that behind me for the next forty-five minutes.

Entertainers have the daunting task of shutting out "real life" when it is show time. Whether it's a comedy show or presenting *The Magic of Life*, I owe it to the people in those seats to do the best I can.

Somehow, I summoned enough strength to get through the program; considering my mental state. The students were amazing and made my job a lot easier. I felt good about the program that we would use for the new video, but I was so emotionally drained when I was done.

I was supposed to go to my girlfriend's place for the weekend. Instead, I had to focus on making travel arrangements to see my aunt in Florida. I feared I would repeat what happened with my grandfather and she would pass away before I could say my goodbye in person. Luckily my cousin, Randy from New York and I were coordinating our flights to make things easier.

As we arrived at the hospice care facility, Jeff tried to prepare me the best he could.

"I walked into the room, but didn't see Susan, so I walked out and asked the nurse where she was. She said I was in the right room." Jeff said. Be prepared, you will not recognize her." I took a few deep breaths and followed my Cousin Randy into the room. As much as I like telling my brother he is wrong, he was right. In the bed was a woman that surely did not look my aunt.

The last time I saw her was at my brother's 50th surprise birthday party in June 2017. Cancer ravaged her features so much. Her breathing was shallow, about one breath every ten seconds. We told her that we were there and that we loved her. She could not respond. The most important thing we could do was be there for my Uncle Michael. It was just a waiting game now.

Like sister, like brother, my father passed away while no one was there. Aunt Susan did the same while we were grabbing a bite to eat for dinner. We got the call as dinner was winding down and we drove back to the hospice care center.

It is said that our loved ones typically pass away when they are alone, to spare us any of any extra grief. There was no sparing us from this. I never would have imagined her dying just ninety days after my father. She joined her brother and parents. Finally, at peace, and no longer in pain from such a horrible disease.

My aunt fought cancer bravely for eight years. She embraced the challenge and gave it everything she had. She lived to experience everything life had to offer. My Aunt Sue was an inspiration to me.

My aunt and uncle were longtime residents of South Florida before spending years in Illinois, north of Chicago. They enjoyed the cooler temperatures where they could hike and play in the snow. In 2017, they returned to Florida and built their dream house in The Villages.

My Aunt called it "camp life" where they played pickleball, drove their golf cart and just had fun together. She even took up piano lessons and once told me, "I wish I did this earlier; I'm getting pretty good."

I thought it was pretty cool that she started to play the piano because her brother Martin always played, even with his Parkinson's.

When I finally started hiking and biking, Aunt Sue would say, "I'm so glad to see you're taking after your old aunt." She and my uncle met in a bike club, and while they never had children, they really enjoyed life together. My aunt and uncle biked so many miles together, even taking bikes to Europe. She was kind, considerate and a true "nosy aunt", always wanting to know what was going on in my life. I will miss her advice whether it be about getting out of debt faster or dating.

Aunt Sue would always end her phone messages to me and Jeff with, "I hope you're out having fun."

As we left the hospice care center, I looked up into the clear night sky and noticed that it was almost a full moon. There appeared to be a double halo around the moon with stars sparkling around it. I couldn't take my eyes off it as we wandered over to the parking lot. It was beautiful to see, and I said, "It's a sign from my dad and Susan that they are okay. They are at peace."

We contacted the same Rabbi who officiated my dad's memorial service. When we saw him again, he offered a smile and said, "It's nice to see you all again, just not under these circumstances. No family should have to go through two deaths so close together."

The cancer had changed Susan so much we didn't know if we should have a last viewing. My uncle agreed to having one and I was glad to have one final goodbye with her. Since I came from Florida, the only thing I had with me to put in her casket was a *The Magic of Life* wristband. She was so supportive I thought it was appropriate.

The Rabbi led another beautiful service. We were joined by some of Susan's New York friends, my cousins Jay and Randy, and her boyfriend Steven. Everyone who spoke about Susan highlighted such precious memories of her amazing spirit. This time Jeff did not give the Rabbi his eulogy. Instead he read a beautiful piece about our aunt. I wanted something that would sum up Susan the best and found the words from a Facebook post that she wrote on October 13, 2016:

New hip (Seven weeks old now) have been cleared to play pickleball and I've played twice already. I was afraid that after five months off the court, I wouldn't remember how to play, but it's coming back to me. The doc told me not to overdo, but as much as I try, it's a very challenging concept for me to understand. I'm so very happy to be pain-free and am able to do the simple things as well as get back on the pickleball courts. It's the simple things that really get me going - doesn't take much to make me happy.

As everyone walked back to their cars, I stayed behind at the family grave site. I looked at the fresh mounds of dirt that were my father and aunt's final resting place. Tears rolled down my face and I started to tremble uncontrollably. I felt alone. Who would I call if I needed advice? Who was going to call me now and check up on how I was doing?

My comedian mind noticed that there were only two more plots left at the grave site. My uncle wants to be buried next to my aunt which leaves one spot. Doing the math, that leaves one remaining spot. *Would it be for my brother or for me? I'm pretty competitive, but I am sure I don't I want to win this competition any time soon.*

It made me chuckle at the fact that I was so worried about where I was to be buried. Forty-seven years ago, I was almost in that plot myself.

I flew back to Ohio the day after her burial and was totally depleted. I just wanted to keep the curtains drawn and let my apartment stay in darkness; which pretty much reflected my mood. Instead of staying home, my girlfriend and I were heading to Colorado for vacation. I tried to put a positive spin on the trip and hoped that the sunny skies and mountain air would be good for us. I won't air our problems to respect her privacy, but on the first day in the Rocky Mountain state the cracks in our relationship began to show. Part of me wanted to just repack and leave immediately, but my aunt loved the outdoors and trails, so I thought I had to complete this trip for her, not for me.

Although my girlfriend and I had our moments of laughter on the trip, we just didn't feel like "us" after the first day. We both embraced the scenery of the Rocky Mountains with our cameras, which was a nice thing to share. When we struggled on a trail, I thought of my dad and aunt who didn't give up, so I pushed through it. We were both going through issues and I know I could have handled it differently. My physical pain made me avoid my mental pain. We may have been together, but I never felt more alone inside. As we flew back to her home in Detroit, I felt the darkness and emptiness in my heart. It was the start of my downward spiral to rock bottom.

Have some laughs with our Aunt Sue

With my Aunt Sue and Uncle Mike at Jeff's surprise 50th
birthday part. 6/24/18

Chapter 32

"Your foundation is broken"

I drove home from her place on Mother's Day afternoon. That annual holiday is bittersweet for me because I never had the chance to know my mother, but yet, I have Dolly. I tried to be a good boyfriend that day and had lunch with her kids, her sister and mother. But I just wanted to get home where I could be alone.

I had only been home only once in the last two weeks. I wanted to get back home and pull the covers over my head. At the same time, I didn't want to burden her with all my heavy feelings. She had a lot going on in her life too.

I drove along I-80 East feeling the pain inside me. I contemplated a lot of things, including driving my car into the concrete divider to put me out of my misery. I thought about my father, my aunt and, now, the possible the end of my relationship.

In retrospect the vacation was a bad idea due to the recent events in our lives. I just didn't feel like me anymore. In fact, I just stopped feeling altogether.

"I think we should break-up." I said a few days after we returned.

I'm not saying it was the right thing to do, but my decision-making skills were pretty bad during this time. The timing of the breakup was horrible because she was also an integral part of the fundraiser for The Magic of Life Foundation which was to be held on June 8th.

After some heavy discussions, she decided to still come to the fundraiser. I was glad because in truthfulness, she worked hard on it. I just wanted the event to go well and for her to see the finished product.

Someone said to me, "You couldn't wait until after the event to break up?" I thought that would have been wrong to do. I was already stressed, not only because of the fundraiser, but because my father's birthday was approaching. I was struggling to make it from one day to the next.

On Wednesday, May 30th, my fellow comedian friend, Greg Smrdel and I met with a counselor from the Kelly's Grief Center located in Kent, Ohio. Greg, along with another fellow comedian, Brian O'Connell, and I developed a program called, *Stand up to Grief.* Greg lost his first wife to breast cancer, Brian lost his son in a motorcycle accident and well, you know my story. We thought about a unique program geared towards men who are going through grief.

As we know, men don't like talking about grief. Let's face it men usually cry two times in our lives: one, at the end of *Field of Dreams* when father and son are playing catch and two, when our favorite sports team wins the championship. We wanted a creative way to share our experiences, and hopefully other men would talk about theirs. We were going to share our stories and then do stand-up comedy to help break the tension of grief. Men feel grief but are so afraid to talk about it because "men aren't supposed to show weakness."

The counselor had known me for years and could sense something was wrong. She knew about the recent deaths in my life and reminded me that if I needed to talk to someone, to make an appointment. In typical Michael fashion, I just nodded and said, "Okay, thanks, I will think about it." I sounded like my father. Over the next two days I had thoughts of "doing something stupid" and made an appointment with her for the upcoming week. It was a huge step toward admitting that I had a major problem.

I remember, in the fall of 2016, I ended a relationship after a few months, because once again I was depressed. Throughout my life I have been good at a few things, like making people laugh, and pushing people away, especially in relationships. I didn't have the necessary tools to cope and thought it would be better to be hated by breaking up with someone, rather than being mourned if I did something stupid. I had built up such a huge wall up around me. I was driving people away that cared about me. I'm not saying it was right, but it was what I did. No one was getting over this wall. No one!

Several factors were contributing to my depression at the time. Work was causing a lot of stress, and I started writing about my mother and Big John for the first time. In 2016, I contributed to two books for the Grief Diaries series, *Through the Eyes of Men - True stories about Loss and Grief from the Male Perspective* and *Hit by an Impaired Driver*. It was extremely scary to write in the books because I was sharing things I never shared before, even on stage. While writing was therapeutic, it also exposed how vulnerable I was when it came to the impact of their deaths. It scared me and I didn't know how to properly cope.

Aunt Sue read the books and said, "I had no idea it impacted you so much as a child. We just thought you were okay."

I am not sure if my father ever read the books, he just marked my "author page" that had my picture and a short bio. I think he just liked telling his friends that I was in two books. He never once mentioned what I had written in them.

With these feelings and emotions bubbling to the surface along with the stress from work, it was a perfect storm. The university had six free counseling sessions and I went twice. Twice! I thought, *you got this, you don't need any counseling.* I was not honest with myself and not ready to deal with the issues.

I was being a typical male when it came to depression, stuffing it way deep down like the seat belts in those old cars. I pretended things were fine. I felt I was better off on my own to handle everything. I did a few things that made me forget about depression, such as hiking and taking pictures with my cell phone.

I have met many people who have become friends through me presenting *The Magic of Life*. One such person is my friend Rae who brought me to speak at Bluffton College a few years ago. As a counselor and photographer, she recommended that I get a camera for when I was out getting "nature therapy" on my hikes. I purchased a refurbished Canon upon her recommendation and found myself channeling my father's passion. While I was out on the trails, I would forget about my internal pain for a bit and submerged myself in the creativity behind the lens. I replaced the negative energy with the positive energy of nature. Like with writing jokes and performing comedy, seeing my pictures afterward gave me the same high. I enjoyed that people liked my pictures as much as I did.

I thought of those memories as I sat in Kelly's Grief Center. I stared down at the intake form and looked over the list of "symptoms" related to depression. I checked off nearly everything on the page. If it was a test, I would have earned an A. Lack of sleep? Yup! Change in appetite? Yup! Irritable? Yup! Thoughts of harming yourself? Yup!

The check marks just continued. I never felt so much internal pain before, and I just wanted it to stop. In previous times, I would think of the dream I had in my 20s about my mom and Big John kicking down the fence. I thought about how his death affected me and that would help steer me away from "doing anything stupid." But this time, it had zero impact. I just wanted all the pain to stop.

Now *The Magic of Life* fundraiser was just days away and instead of being full of excitement and proud of what a little-known organization was about to do, I wanted to die.

I had no idea if I was going to make it to the fundraiser and that scared the shit out of me. Even my sense of humor was gone, the one thing I used as a defense mechanism was gone. I struggled to leave my apartment and I felt the weight of the world on my shoulders. It was exhausting pretending I was "okay."

I had my first counseling session on June 5th, the same day Kate Spade committed suicide. I didn't know the woman or what she did, yet her death still affected me. Throughout the day I kept on repeating to myself, "Don't let that be you. Fight this."

Talking about what I was going through was awfully scary. But at the same time, knowing my counselor for so many years was a little comforting, because it wasn't some total stranger. She cared about me and I trusted her.

She asked me if I had a plan to do harm to myself and I lied. With the fundraiser days away, I was afraid that if I said yes, I would be sent away to be evaluated. It was my name on the line for the event. I had to be there, so yeah, I started off counseling with a lie. I told her I had thoughts of harming myself but no plan. But yes, I had a plan.

My grandfather once said he wanted the Dr. Kevorkian treatment when he was having health issues. At this point and time in my life, I wished for the same thing. Robin Williams, if you remember, was a huge comedy influence on me, and I thought about how he took his own life. As I sat in my office with the door closed, I stared at my brown sweater hanging up on the wall.

I then stared at the doorknob and thought, "Well, I can pull the shades down, have my back against the door, no one can see inside behind the door through the little window. By the time people would wonder where I am, it will be too late. My body will be against the door, they wouldn't be able to push through."

I stared at the sweater, then the door. Stared at the sweater, then the door. I put my head on my desk, closed my eyes and took a few deep breaths. Hell, I wasn't even sure the sweater could get the job done, but it is all I had at that moment.

As I was taking those breaths I thought of Dolly and Jeff. I just couldn't do it to them. Dolly's sister passed away after my father and she was dealing with so much. How could I do that to her? My brother would also be devastated. How could I do that to him and send him back to the cemetery for a third trip?

I stood up, opened the door and went for a walk. I had to get out of my office. If I didn't, you would not be reading this book. The pain was pulsating through every fiber of my body and I had to find a way to make it stop.

Three days after Kate Spade died by suicide, Anthony Bourdain took his life. It was on June 8th, the same day as the fundraiser. I read all the news stories about Kate Spade and him dying. All the articles said, "Why did they do this? How come they didn't get help?" The articles included signs of depression and I had all of them; which I already knew. I didn't want people that cared about me to ask the same thing. I just kept on telling myself, "Don't let that be you, fight it, think of Dolly and Jeff, your other family members, your friends. Your dad and aunt would want you to fight." I was a nervous wreck for the event not to mention I would also be seeing my ex-girlfriend for the first time in over a month. I had no idea how *that* was going to go either.

At the fundraiser, we were presenting awards to nine officers and presenting the first ever "Marty Gershe" award to Judge Hoover. I had to keep on pretending I was fine. It was exhausting. My dear friend Rae, who is a wonderful photographer, volunteered to take new headshots of me and capture the event. I was not in a "smiling mood" for the pictures, but I did need new ones. When Rae reviewed the pictures after the event she said,

"We need to take new ones, your eyes look so sad. This is not the Michael I know. You don't have that sparkle in your eyes." I guess you can't fool a camera. No one knew how close I was to ending my life that week. The pain of all the grief weighed like two tons on my shoulders.

The event was incredible, and everyone enjoyed the evening. Despite this, I did not enjoy the moment because of the way I was feeling. I had so much anxiety. It prevented me from appreciating the fundraiser. My friends who performed brought a lot of laughter and people were already talking about "next year" as soon as we were done. I emceed the event, but I did not want any of the spotlight. That was for the Judge, the officers, and my friends performing. The Judge turned the tables on me and talked about *The Magic of Life* and the impact it had on the offenders. With my emotions so frayed, I nearly started to cry as he spoke.

We are not MADD, we don't have huge corporate sponsors to assist with the cost, but we had such a great evening. I felt proud to give recognition to our men and women on the front line trying to take drunk drivers off the road. I was also grateful and humbled that a former

Ashland teammate who was also a retired police officer donated a nice sum to help cover some of the costs. The event ran smoothly and while people left happy, I was just happy that the night was finally over. Before driving home, I sat in my car, exhausted and alone in my thoughts. I was sad that I couldn't call my father or aunt to let them know how it all went. It actually took me a few days to be proud of what we accomplished.

Sitting outside on my balcony later that night, I confessed to my ex-girlfriend the thoughts I was having. She admitted that she was worried about me. It was very emotional for the both of us. Naturally I told her, "I won't do anything stupid; I promise." I hoped that was a promise I could fulfill. She suggested medication, but I wanted to see what I could do with grief therapy before rushing to take any pills. I'm not against medication, but I needed to work the problem first. I was the problem. We talked for a long time to see if we could work things out, but my mind was so much in a fog, I just wanted to wake up the next day.

As we laid in bed that night, I started to cry uncontrollably. Everything that was causing my pain: my dad, my aunt, the stress of the fundraiser, the uncertainty of my relationship, and my thoughts of ending my life, came pouring out. The water works wouldn't stop, and I kept on saying, "What is wrong with me?" It was now five months after my father's death and two after my aunt's. I realized I had never begun to grieve. I was broken and this time I couldn't pretend that everything was fine.

The next morning, as she slept, I went outside and called Dolly to let her know how the fundraiser went. I also told her what I've been going through. She gave me the best advice a mother could give her son. "Your foundation is broken and before you can be with someone, you have to fix your foundation." Once again, Dolly was right and no matter how painful it was, between the long distance, and other things in the relationship, I had to take care of myself first and foremost.

I am not going to air our dirty laundry, but I believed that my ex and I both had to focus on issues within our own worlds. It was not easy to officially end the relationship. She was angry but I didn't feel I could work on myself and the relationship at the same time. I had to put myself first. She also said that she would not wait for me as I started grief therapy. That was fair because who knew how long it would take?

My father never talked about death or grief and I didn't want to emulate that characteristic of him anymore. I did not want to carry the weight of all that grief on my shoulders anymore, either. I was tired of pretending I was okay. I needed the time and energy to put the work into healing because my life depended on it.

Chapter 33

Fixing my foundation

I promised myself that I would do whatever it took in grief therapy to stop the pain I was feeling. I needed to start the healing process. This would not be just two sessions like in the past. I was in it for the long haul. I was determined to fix my foundation.

One of the first questions in my second appointment was, "Did you ever grieve for your mom as a child?" The counselor also asked, "Do you think her death impacted your relationships?" I was like wait a second, "I'm here to talk about my dad and aunt." But she was right, those were important questions to answer, and for the first time in life, it was time not to avoid the impact of my mother's death.

As a kid, I was happy being in my own little world of Star Wars battles, engrossed in Spider-man comics, pretending to be James Bond or a fifth member of KISS— don't judge. You've come too far in this book to start judging me now. Plus, swimming took up so much time, who had time to even think about grief? I had to make sure my swim suit was tied! My escape in those worlds helped me avoid reality. Those worlds were much safer to be in, even as an adult. As an avid reader, I would sink myself into fantasy worlds of literary heroes such as Bond, Mitch Rapp, Jack Reacher, and Alex Cross. Flawed characters who, in a violent world, saved the day.

But as a kid, no, I never grieved for my mother. My father didn't talk about her, there was no counseling. Everyone thought I was fine. I didn't have the developmental skills to question her death or more importantly, understand it as a kid. I excelled in using my creativity as an escape and it carried over into adulthood because it's where I felt safe.

Sometimes I get asked, "How come you are not married or have kids?" Well, my married friends tell me not to get married, so I try to be a good friend. Actually, for a long time, dating wasn't a huge priority. When I was younger, I was focused on comedy. Dating was put on the back burner. I concentrated on my dreams. To be honest, what kept me away from long term relationships the most, is that I saw how my mother's death affected my father, and that scared me.

I saw the pain my father went through with the death of my mother. Family members told me he was never the same after her death. In an email from him on December 19, 2012 which would have been their 48th wedding anniversary, he wrote, *"Maybe I should have mentioned things about your Mother to you before, but the pain has been too great, even after all these years and has been something I have had to endure. I guess I just never got over losing her and kept it within me."*

I never wanted to experience that pain, so I put up an incredible wall around me like a security blanket. Even though I've been in relationships, I never let anyone really see me. I was too scared. I wasn't letting anyone in no matter what. I wanted to protect myself. Even if it meant a lonely life. I'd rather be alone than to face the same hell my father lived. Right or wrong, it is what I did to protect myself, and it all stemmed from not properly grieving for my mother's death.

I was just afraid to experience that type of loss, so I closed off my emotions. But now with grief therapy, I was understanding myself a lot better. By discussing my mother's death and the effect it had on me, I had to let go of that fear, otherwise, I would spend the rest of my life alone. I could feel the wall was coming down. Cue Ronald Reagan, "TEAR DOWN THIS WALL!" I am quite confident that when I do enter my next relationship, the wall will not be there, and I feel happy about that.

It took me forty-eight years to realize that the car crash does not define who I am. I used to think it was one-hundred-percent of who I was, but it's not. It was such a burden. It will always be a part of me, but now I know it shouldn't make up my entire being. What can I say? I'm a slow learner.

When I told a former student from grad school and longtime friend, Rebecca, I was attending grief therapy she shouted, "Thank God! About time! I'm so happy for you! You carry your mother's death and John's on your shoulders all the time." Feeling that pressure come off my shoulders was such a huge relief. It was like finally exhaling after holding my breath for forty-eight years.

With each weekly session, another layer was stripped away. I was focused on fixing my foundation. Instead of reading my favorite authors to escape reality with, I started reading Tony Robbins, Brene Brown and

Mark Manson. I never read any self-help books before, but I couldn't get enough of them now. Tony Robbins taught me that I control how I react to certain things. When my birthday rolled around and I didn't get that call from my aunt or dad, instead of being depressed, I thought of joyful memories that I shared with them on my previous birthdays.

I looked at the card my father gave me last year where he wrote he was proud of me. Yes, I was sad, but instead of being depressed, I decided to appreciate the memories. I was learning that there is a difference between feeling sad and being depressed. In my depressed states, I could feel my serotonin levels drop, and I would withdraw from everyone and everything. When I only felt sadness, I didn't feel that physical difference and it wasn't so devastating. Sadness was a temporary feeling.

I also found myself crying a lot more, letting those emotions that were sealed up for so long, flow. Brene Brown taught me that it's okay to show my vulnerability and that there is no shame in doing so. When I went to see my second favorite band Tesla, in July, I started to cry by the third song. I couldn't control myself, I just let the emotions run free. I didn't want people to see me cry at a rock concert, but I was so appreciative of being alive. I thought, if I had "done something stupid" I wouldn't be here rocking out tonight. Their music meant so much to me. I was living in the moment rather than living in the past—that was a new feeling too.

I started meditating and attempted to do yoga. Just a few minutes of meditation really helped clear my mind and focus on my breathing. In regard to yoga, well, in my mind, my poses were like the pictures in the book, but in reality? I highly doubt anyone is going to ask me how to do the warrior one pose. I also returned to the gym which was something I missed. Sometimes the gym was cruel to me, but I felt so much better after a good workout. There were times where I pushed myself harder in the gym to purge my negative feelings. Healthy mind, body and spirit isn't a lie.

My counselor told me to have daily grief appointments where I would take some time in the day and just let all the emotions come out. Whether I cried or yelled, get it all out. Let those tears just flow until you can't cry anymore. Sometimes I would have them in my car spontaneously. I would think about those who I had lost in my life. Sometimes swearing was involved, so if I was in the car, I turned up my music a little more. It felt wonderful to purge these feelings that I had kept bottled up inside of me.

When I thought of my dad in the hospital room or my aunt in her hospice room, I would be angry at God for making them suffer. It really disrupted any relationship I may have had with a higher power. I've been angry with God before regarding my mother's death, but this time, it was different. I stopped wearing my chai and Star of David shortly after my aunt's passing. My grandparents gave me the chai, which consists of the eighth and tenth letter of the Hebrew alphabet. The letters together mean life and represent being alive. In college, people thought I was wearing a dog or cow on my chain.

At the time I thought, *there is no God*. I had lost my faith after seeing what my loved ones went through. Who can be that cruel? The images of my father and aunt suffering were so vivid. Today my relationship with God still isn't great, but I'm getting there. I'm getting there. Sadly, it took the shooting at the Pittsburgh synagogue to remind me what it means to be a Jew. I returned my chain back to its proper place around my neck.

Another great tool that I learned in therapy was to write letters to those people in my life that are gone. I wrote to my parents, Aunt Sue, Big John, hell, I even wrote to Harvey. Now, I will admit, the one to Harvey is filled with language that would be banned on tv, radio, and even Facebook, but damn, it felt good to get that anger out! I wrote to my family members as if I was writing from camp. I told them how I was feeling, what I was doing in life and that I missed them. I just hoped they could decipher my wonderful handwriting.

Perhaps Grandma Sophie was right after-all, I should have been a doctor the way my handwriting is. But whenever I felt the urge of missing them and knowing I couldn't pick up the phone to talk to them, I wrote a letter.

I miss my dad calling and saying, "Hello Michael, it's me, Dad." I would tease him and say, "Yes, I know it was you, your name comes up on my phone."

Another activity that I learned in counseling which helped get some feelings out was the bean bag throw. My counselor had me pick up different colored bean bags and throw them at a chalkboard. I started to relive a childhood dream of being a Major League Baseball pitcher and threw as hard as I could. The bean bag made a nice "thud" against the board each time. The first time I did it in the office, I focused on Big John. Throwing the bags against the wall allowed me to expel that "dark energy," because I was still mad at him for driving drunk. I actually started to cry when I thought about John.

At home I would use corn-hole bean bags and hurl them against the wall of my garage. I stink at corn-hole, so this was a better use of them anyway. I would throw so hard that after fifteen minutes I would have to ice my shoulder. It was a wonderful exercise that allowed me to vent, but in a healthy way.

I refused to self- medicate during this time because it would only mask the symptoms and I needed to heal properly. Even my counselor was against medication because we had to work the problem – me!

I found myself actually being happy for the first time in I don't know how long. I would have moments of happiness like being at a KISS concert. I'm not saying I was never happy in a relationship, but on a whole, I wasn't. Since I had the wall up in relationships, I protected myself because I never wanted anyone to see the other side of me. Faking all that happiness was so exhausting and now, I was genuinely happy. I found myself smiling in traffic instead of cursing—okay, sometimes I still curse, but I'm happy being alive, even in traffic.

I embraced my hiking with a new sense of enjoyment and took in every sound and sight with more appreciation. When I look through my viewfinder of my camera, my life is much more in focus. I think I am pretty good behind the lens, and I have a different perspective now when I take pictures. Perhaps I inherited my dad's gift for photography after all.

I don't feel so ashamed, or a burden to my friends anymore, as I started to tell some about my situation. They said, "Call whenever you have to" or "Why didn't call me before?" I thought about Kate Spade and Anthony Bourdain and wondered if they knew about their support systems. I can't put into words how much it means to me to have the friends that I do.

I grew accustomed to being so independent in my life. I didn't want to be a burden to anyone, so I kept it all bottled up for so long. I was like a balloon with too much air about to pop with my grief. When I found out that I would not be a burden, I realized how much my actions would have impacted them. It is not time for people to start writing memories of me on my Facebook page.

During my sessions, I would say, "I was thinking of doing something stupid." I was avoiding the ugly truth. My counselor finally got me to say, "I was thinking of killing myself. That I wanted to die by suicide." I didn't want to say that word because it was scary. By saying, "I wanted to do something stupid" instead, it softened it up. We talked about the times I thought about killing myself throughout my life and the reasons why. We also talked about why I didn't kill myself, and how I couldn't do that to my family or my friends. I didn't want them to go through the pain of my death. My counselor said, "A lot of people don't recognize that by committing suicide the impact it will make on others, but you understood the magnitude of it. You realized how it would affect the people that care about you. This time you thought about Dolly and Jeff."

I felt myself returning to that fun, mischievous kid at heart again. I was not hiding behind a wall of pain and it was liberating. Dolly would call me "Michael Finnegan" as a kid after the nursery rhyme because I was a "little goofball" and therapy allowed me to get back to that person. I was truly enjoying life again.

I was caught in a rain storm on a hike. Before counseling I would have been bitching and moaning about being in the rain. But now, I laughed like a little kid and enjoyed every puddle, every stream we crossed. It was like I was reborn.

Grief therapy has also had a huge impact on my programs. I found myself becoming a better presenter without carrying all that weight of grief. I was at peace and having more fun presenting the program; which the audience picked up on. I no longer felt so emotionally drained by carrying the ghost of my mother and Big John on my shoulders. I am not afraid to let the audience see the darkness because someone else could be going through the same thing. I want to inspire people to get help if they need it. There is no shame in asking for help. And if I can do it with humor, even better.

Throughout my life I have been through every stage of grief: denial, anger, bargaining, acceptance, and depression. With my mother, I never had the denial stage and went right into acceptance as a kid. As I got older it was anger and bargaining. With Big John, I was angry for so long because I felt betrayed by him. There was a little denial until I saw him at the wake and then acceptance hit me. When my grandfather passed away, acceptance hit me first because my father told me in the car as we left the airport. And then this year with the double whammy of my father and aunt, each stage could change within a minute. There was denial with the fact both were really gone and then anger directed at God for making them suffer.   Throughout my therapy, I realized that I was depressed for much of my life. I learned I hid behind it with humor. All this grief on my shoulders, every single day. With the death of my mother occurring when it did, I was pretty much born into the world of grief and was left alone to figure it out on my own until now. No wonder I had this huge wall around me. I just continued through life thinking, "Well this is how my life is supposed to be."

I realize now, it doesn't have to be. Asking for help is not a weakness by any means, it's a strength. I remember my father when he asked if I needed a math tutor. I had to swallow my pride and say yes. Otherwise I never would have made it out of my algebra class. Likewise, I never would have made it out of the pain of depression if I didn't ask for help.

At one of our final sessions, my counselor said, "You seem like a different person. You even look different." And this is from someone who has known me for years.

I said, "I am. For the first time in many, many years, I am truly happy. I feel really good about myself." Not to slight people in past relationships, but only we can make ourselves happy. I know my next relationship will be a lot different whenever that might be.

Knowing my past admittance of "faking happiness", she asked, "Are you faking it or are you really happy?"

I thought if I was this good of an actor, I would have stayed a theater major in college. "No, I can't fake this, I feel such a difference in myself as well. I really am happy. I've finally found peace within myself."

As a toddler, I was "tossed" into the pool. I learned how to survive in the water without drowning. Sure, we may cry a lot at the thought of getting into the water, but the object is not to drown. Besides the instructor won't let us either. Not drowning is such a powerful image to me because throughout my life, I've tried not to drown. Whether it be in school, relationships (and I've drowned some in great fashion), comedy, speaking, or on a day to day basis, the thought of drowning is terrifying. I've come to realize as an adult, I've come close to drowning, but yet, I find a way to "swim" and get to the wall. At the wall I can rest and just breathe until I push off for another lap. Life is just a series of swimming laps. Sometimes my head is just above the water line, and when I feel myself about to go under, I kick and pull, and breathe.

As long as I remember to just swim, with my suit tied of course, I should be okay. Didn't Dory say that as well? "Just keep swimming?"

I feel that my depression no longer controls me and that I am a survivor of it. I have been a survivor my entire life. There is a quote from Carl Jung that I recently started to use in *The Magic of Life* that really speaks to me, "*I am not what has happened to me. I am what I choose to become.*" Sometimes we may not be able to control what happens to us, but we can control how it affects us. Take it from a guy who probably should have died at eight weeks old due to a drunk driver. No matter how bad you think it is, you have a chance to live an amazing life. We have the power to decide how we will live our lives, not someone else.

Close your eyes once again, feel your pulse, that heartbeat—THAT'S AMAZING! If you can feel your pulse, you can live your dreams. That, my friends, is the magic of life!

The End

Made in the USA
Monee, IL
20 January 2021